ALASKA GOLD
Life on the New Frontier, 1898 - 1906

Dear Mother —

Will write tonight as there is a vessel going out in a day or two. We received father's letter of Aug 28 and Lulu's of a few days earlier. They came in on the Ohio. We are still having very unusual weather. The weather took a sudden notion to freeze up a few days ago and so now we are having — — — — The night — — — — around 25° — — — — oze all day. — — — — north with — — — — eau. Skati — — — — one if it — — — — and — — — — — had ditches — — — — the usually — — — — — we last — — it seems to have come to stay. Last night we had another fine

---

Mr J. J. McDaniel
Cor. Union & Naglee
San Jose, Cal.

UDAKT JUN 13 1900 ALASKA

ALASKA GOLD

Life on the New Frontier, 1898 - 1906

Letters and Photographs of the McDaniel Brothers

Edited by Jeff Kunkel

Centennial Edition

Scottwall Associates, Publishers
with the
California Historical Society
San Francisco
1997

Library of Congress Catalog Card Number: 97-67656

Cataloging in Publication Data:
Kunkel, Jeff.
    Alaska Gold: Life on the New Frontier, 1898-1906. Photographs and
    Letters of the McDaniel Brothers. Edited by Jeff Kunkel.
    1. Nome, Alaska—1898-1906.   2. Gold mining.   3. McDaniel, Wilfred, Sr.
    4. McDaniel, Edmund.   5. McDaniel, Jessie Drake.   6. Alaska natives.
    7. Siberia. 8. San Jose, California.

Book and cover design: James Heig
Editor: Jeff Kunkel

First Edition: 5 4 3 2 1
Copyright ©1997 Jeff Kunkel

Scottwall Associates, Publishers
95 Scott Street
San Francisco, CA 94117
Telephone (415) 861-1956

All rights reserved. No part of this book may be reproduced in any form or by any electronic or mechanical means, including information storage and retrieval systems, without permission in writing from the publisher, except by a reviewer, who may quote brief passages.

Printed in the U.S.A.

ISBN 0-942087-14-3

In loving memory of
Wilfred McDaniel Sr.
Edmund McDaniel
Jessie Drake McDaniel

Acknowledgments

This book is the result of one hundred years of collaboration between many generous and talented people.

I am deeply grateful to Wilfred, Sr., Edmund, and Jessie McDaniel for documenting their lives on the New Frontier with such rigor and craft.

I thank their descendants, Wilfred McDaniel, Jr., and his wife Lois; Irene McDaniel Johnson and her husband, Robert Johnson; Esther McDaniel, and Ruth Fontaine for long cherishing and now generously sharing this work.

I also thank the artists, scholars, and photographers who have helped shape and present this work, especially Larry Sultan, Iris Davis, Lucas Feltzman, Ross Van der Horn, Doug McCoy, Richard Orsi, Kevin Starr, Nelson Graburn, and Ira Jacknis.

Finally, I thank those who have helped this work become a book and a traveling exhibit, especially James Heig, Michael McCone, Emily Wolff, Bo Mampho, Marian Ueke, and the editorial board of the California Historical Society.

Table of Contents

Foreword ix
Introduction 1
California Ranch 7
Sea Legs 11
Dutch Harbor 23
Through the Ice Floes 35
Nome, the New Frontier 43
Mining 55
Storms 75
Home 85
Neighbors 95
Siberia 115
Sundays 125
Winter 141
Epilogue 163

Cape Nome Alaska Sept 2.

Dear Folks.

To day is stormy so that we cannot work. The sea is rolling very high and the wind & rain keep us all inside. Yesterday was a beautiful day. The sun shone all day and the sea calm. We did good day started a few had on accou We finish I have mo

J. J. McDaniel Esq.
San Jose
Cal.

Naglee
and
Union Ave.

Foreword

No one region has ever held the collective imagination of Northern California and the San Francisco Bay Area more dramatically than Alaska. One arm of Alaska—Russian California—extended down to Fort Ross and San Francisco Bay, and even down the coast to Monterey Bay, where the Fort Ross-based Aleut hunters sometimes took their kayaks in pursuit of sea otter.

The reverberations of Russian California maintained their strength down through the nineteenth century, and were given even further momentum at the turn of the century in the fiction of Gertrude Atherton. The love story, as Atherton envisioned it, involving the Sitka-based Russian entrepreneur Count Nikolai Petrovich Rezanov and Concepcion Argüello, daughter of the commandant of the San Francisco Presidio, bespoke in human terms the enduring connection between an Alaska that once belonged to Russia and a California that once belonged to Spain.

California and the territory of Alaska were both brought precipitously into the Union by action of the federal government: the Mexican War, in which the United States claimed California by right of conquest, and the purchase of Alaska in 1867, during the brief administration of President Andrew Johnson, by Secretary of State William Henry Seward, for the bargain basement price of $7.2 million. In each instance, the direct action of a single figure, President Polk in the Mexican War and Secretary Seward in the Alaska purchase, abruptly annexed a vast and largely unknown region on the Pacific.

When gold was discovered on Anvil Creek near Nome, Alaska, in 1898, fifty years after the discovery of gold in California, Northern Californians had an opportunity to relive the foundational event of California itself, the Gold Rush. The 1890s in Northern California, especially the second half of the decade, were very much about the recovery of the frontier. Historian Frederick Jackson Turner announced to the American Historical Society, meeting at the Columbian Exposition in Chicago in 1893, that for all practical purposes the frontier was finished. Young California was deeply concerned over losing the energy and drive of two earlier frontier generations. In one sense, the anxiety was part of a national trend (Theodore

Roosevelt, Frederic Remington, and Owen Wister, among others, felt it most intensely). But the anxiety had a special Northern California dimension as the region began to experience rapid urbanization around San Francisco Bay. Within a few short years, more than half the population of the state would be living in cities or suburbs on the shores of San Francisco Bay. Northern California in the 1890s was in a period of transition between the frontier past and the metropolitan future.

That, for one reason, is why the emergent writers of the period—Frank Norris and Jack London come immediately to mind—so prized what Theodore Roosevelt would eventually call The Strenuous Life. In Jack London's case, the Klondike Gold Rush provided the moral and imaginative matrix, the galvanizing occasion, for his emergent talent. In London's *The Call of the Wild* (1903), the story opens in the sunny Santa Clara Valley and moves to the glacial ferocity of the Far North. The McDaniel brothers and Ed McDaniel's wife, Jessie Drake McDaniel, experience a similar transition from the genteel to the primordial. The McDaniel family ranch in San Jose, in fact, could have served as the setting for the opening portions of London's great novel.

Epic events such as the Nome Gold Rush, which drew the McDaniels north, are usually remembered through the prisms of either formal history or imaginative art. Thus, for example, the Klondike and Yukon fiction of Jack London, one of the most popular writers of modern times, together with a handful of first-rate histories, has fixed irretrievably the structure and content of the Klondike Gold Rush as recoverable and recovered epic. Yet many of the men and women of the nineteenth century wrote their own history, privately, through diaries, journals and letters.

In the case of the California Gold Rush, no single imaginative work of art, in fact, can be said to surpass in value or intensity the diaries, journals, and letters of the period. These documents, over the past half century, have been recovered from the archives, edited and published. Today it is this literature of fact and observation, rather than the more slender fiction and poetry of the era, which constitutes the central and enduring epic of this transforming social event.

In the nineteenth century (and well into the twentieth century as well), a great number of Americans—educated or not—were capable of direct and vivid observation and wrote well enough to transform those observations into a distinctive sort of literature. Obviously, the McDaniel brothers were possessed of this ability, as the letters in this volume vividly attest. Here in all their specificity are the facts, sights, sounds, smells and engaging detail of this Far North frontier at the turn of the century.

Then there is the question of the camera. Recent criticism has traced the rapid emergence of photography in the mid-nineteenth century as a high art form. It was an art form, moreover, that proved especially accessible to ordinary Americans such as Wilfred McDaniel, whose stunning photographs are central to the power and force of this volume. Frontier California showed a distinct affinity for photography as a means of both workaday documentation and artistic expression. The great California photographer Carleton Watkins, for example, the Walt Whitman of California photography, if you will, did not view himself primarily as an artist, despite the high art of so many of his photographs, but as a working man busy about a thousand photographic tasks, from passport pictures to the documentation of mining practices, cityscapes, ranch life, and shipwrecks.

Wilfred McDaniel, one suspects, had a similar unself-conscious attitude towards his photography. Yet look at the result! Here are images of the Nome frontier as clear and direct, in their own terms, as the descriptions of Jack London.

There is an austerity in these images, a minimalism even, a lack of fussiness, in powerful synergy with the unpretentious strength of the letters.

Here, then, is a volume of spontaneous, unpretentious art. Here is an epic as experienced and expressed by Californians employing the almost demotic tools of letters and photographs: modes of art and expression available, if not to the masses, then to men and women of ordinary means in that time a century ago. The McDaniels did not set forth in search of art. They wanted gold. But the art came nevertheless, and in this volume, some forty to fifty years after their deaths and nearly a hundred years after their great adventure, they truly strike it rich.

—Kevin Starr, Ph. D.
California State Librarian

Wilfred A. McDaniel
1874 - 1954

Edmund J. McDaniel
1872 - 1951

Jessie A. (Drake) McDaniel
1870 - 1947

Introduction

WILFRED AND EDMUND MCDANIEL left their California ranch in the first year of the twentieth century, boarded a steamship in San Francisco, sailed north and west for twenty-five days, staked a mining claim on a desolate Bering Sea beach, and for six years lived as gold miners on America's New Frontier, Alaska. This book honors the Centennial anniversary of the Nome Gold Rush, a tumultuous migration which included thousands of prospectors from California and around the world.

The brothers and their sister, Lulu, were born to Josiah and Amanda McDaniel and raised on their parents' apricot ranch in San Jose. Josiah, a Confederate officer, had come to California from Kentucky shortly after the Civil War. Amanda was a forty-niner, having come west by wagon train from Missouri as an infant in 1849. As boys, Will and Ed first mined for gold near their San Jose ranch. Will wrote:

> Ed and I were camping in the Santa Cruz Mountains, hunting and fishing, when we made the acquaintance of Antonio, a mixture of Spanish and Indian blood common in California at the time when the '49ers arrived by ox-teams. Antonio was mining in the streambed, using a small sluice and working the sand and gravel, and he taught me to pan. The yellow flake in my first pan became the germ of a mining career of many years. The chance meeting with Antonio, and the resulting interest in his work, expanded like the proverbial ripple on the pool, after the stone is thrown, taking me to all the mining regions of California and ultimately to the far north, across the Bering Sea to the shores of Asia, where on its desolate wastes I recalled the fact that small beginnings may take us—we know not where.*

Before the discovery of gold in the far north, the Alaska frontier drew only a handful of people from the states—whalers, missionaries, salmon fishermen, and reindeer herders. In the 1890s, southeast Alaska began to attract wealthy Americans for hunting, fishing, and sightseeing excursions. In 1896, the discovery of gold along Canada's Klondike River drew thousands of prospectors into southeast Alaska on their way to the Klondike and brought the territory of Alaska to the forefront of America's attention. The McDaniel brothers closely followed the news out of the Klondike, but they stayed in California, working on their ranch and at their father's placer mine in Trinity County, California.

---

* All quotations without footnotes are from the writings of the McDaniel brothers.

In 1898 gold was discovered near Nome, Alaska. Will, in his memoirs, wrote,

> Following close upon the heels of the great Klondike gold-rush, news of gold discoveries in the Cape Nome area of the Seward Penninsula began trickling out to "the States." The great stampede to Nome was on! Gold in the creeks, gold in the benches. Even the sands of the seashore gleamed with the yellow flakes!

The gold on the beaches had arrived by stream and river erosion, but many miners believed that the bottom of the Bering Sea was covered with gold. "It was a poor miner's dream come true: a land where the gold apparently came in with the tide like driftwood."[1] These miners came to be called Sourdoughs, because many brought bottles of sourdough starter for their biscuit and bread dough. Ed joined the stampede in 1899; Will in 1900.

Most prospectors boarded steamships in Seattle or San Francisco in May or June and began a three-thousand-mile sea voyage which could last a month and was often fraught with hardship—overcrowding, disease, poor food, cold, violence, gales, and ice floes. Will wrote,

> We were just packed in the hold like cattle. Most of the steerage were foreigners and dirty as hogs. When they were seasick they just vomited on the floor . . . It was only the cold climate that kept down a pestilence.

Ships routinely stopped for coal and food in Dutch Harbor, a deep water harbor on Unalaska Island in the Aleutian Archipelago. So many ships were damaged or sunk by Bering Sea ice that ship captains had to get permission from their insurers to leave Dutch Harbor and enter the Bering Sea. During his first trip into the Bering Sea, Will wrote, "If a gale should come up while we are in the ice...we would go to the bottom as the ice would crush our boat like an egg shell."

From the Nome anchorage, Ed wrote, "We are soon to be dumped off like cattle onto the cold bleak coast of Nome." The brothers, like most Sourdoughs, had never experienced anything like the environment of the Seward Peninsula—black and ruby sand beaches covered with snow for nine months a year, permanently frozen earth below a thin layer of soil, treeless tundra carpeted with wildflowers and berry bushes in summer, barren foothills, fierce storms, and daylight which varied from less than four hours at the winter solstice to more than twenty hours at the summer solstice. As for winter, Will wrote, "Cold is no name for it." Will and Ed hunted for ptarmigan, fished for trout and tomcod, and purchased dried, salted, or canned food from Nome merchants, several of whom they knew from San Jose. The brothers missed their family and friends, church, trees, and fresh fruit. Ed wrote, "I wish I had some green fruit pretty bad."

Natives, dressed in furs and calico, inhabited tiny villages along the coast. L. H. French, the general manager of the Nome Hydraulic Mining Company, wrote in 1901, "The natives of the Seward Peninsula, numbering about eight hundred, are Eskimo, or as they call themselves, Innuits,"[2] descendants of an ancient people who crossed a land bridge—now under the Bering Sea—from East Cape, Siberia, to Cape Prince of Wales, Alaska. Will wrote, "*Eskimo* . . . is the corruption of a Danish word . . . meaning 'those who eat raw flesh.'" The Russians had settled southeast Alaska as early as the 1700s, but they had never settled northwest Alaska. French wrote, "Prior to the recent discoveries of gold, the only whites on the Seward Pensinsula with whom [the natives] came in contact were the few Americans in charge of the several missions and reindeer stations, and a score or so of Swedes and Lapps employed as herders."3 French does not mention the encounters between the natives and foreign whalers, who often visited native villages from 1860 to 1910. The whalers traded firearms, cartridges, calico, denim, needles, tobacco, liquor, sugar, matches and tools for furs, whalebone, walrus ivory, carvings and sexual favors.

The natives were never interested in gold, but they were interested in the goldseekers. This association brought opportunity and catastrophe. In 1901, Will wrote:

There are a great many Eskimos here this year. They come from as far as the Arctic and from the islands, Diomedes and St. Lawrence. They are trading ivory and mucklucks and drinking all the whiskey they can get.

Whole families, even villages, died of consumption and pneumonia, "before which their constitutions seem to be helpless."4 George Bird Grinnell, an ethnologist on the Harriman Expedition of 1899, wrote,

White men...swarm over the Alaska coast, and are overwhelming the Eskimo. They have taken away their women, and debauched the men with liquor. They have brought them strange new diseases that they never knew before, and in a very short time they will ruin and disperse the wholesome, hearty, merry people we saw. 5

In 1904, the United States government established a reservation near Nome to assist sick native peoples. Will was initially put off by the Eskimos who lived near his claim and wrote, "They are a shiftless lot and take life easy." But he gradually grew interested in his native neighbors; he collected their tools, wrote about their ways, even learned their language.

NOME, created by the Sourdoughs in 1898, became Alaska's largest city by 1900, home to one-third of all the whites living in Alaska. French wrote,

As late as July, 1899, Nome City was nothing but a city of tents. By the first of August, over fifty buildings had been erected . . . in a very short space of time Front Street was lined with shops, saloons, dance halls, gambling houses, and restaurants. 6

This was no small feat, since all lumber had to be shipped in or scavenged from shipwrecks. In the summer of 1900, Will estimated that "there are about 20,000 people at Cape Nome and its vicinity"—but many of the miners returned to the states each winter. There was no regular law enforcement. The population of Nome stabilized in 1905 at about 4,500 residents, its current population—half white, half native (Yup'ik, Siberian Yup'ik, and Inupiaq) Today, the entire Seward Peninsula—45,000 square miles—has only 9,000 residents.

Mining was going on all along the beach near Nome when the brothers arrived. Will wrote, "Just imagine 25 miles of beach covered with tents and people." The McDaniel brothers set up their tent on the beach and began mining about eight miles north of Nome. First, they rocked beach sand, but soon they received a shipment of supplies from Seattle and began to sluice the sand with a gasoline engine, pump, sluice boxes and sea water.

In the early years the brothers returned to

California in the fall. On June 1, 1904, Ed married his sweetheart, Jessie Drake, and the day after the wedding she left with the brothers for Nome, to become one of the few women among the miners. She cooked, mended clothes, cared for their sled dogs, hunted for wildflowers and tundra berries, and hung curtains and wallpaper in the cabin which the brothers built. In 1901, Will and Ed learned how to mine ancient layers of beach sand covered with frozen tundra. They used a technique known as steam thawing, which allowed them to mine throughout the year.

L. H. French wrote, "Nine-tenths of the men who worked plants on the beach made dismal failures, some of the remainder made expenses, and a few happened to find rich spots and made some money."[7]

The McDaniel brothers made some money. On September 16, 1901, Ed wrote to his parents, "We have taken out $3,000 in gold. We have saved up for ourselves, after our expenses, about $1,500." Gold brought $17.50 per troy ounce. The brothers supplemented their income with boat building, engine pump repair—even dentistry, and their journey was followed with great interest in California. An article about them appeared in the *San Jose Mercury News* on June 28th, 1905, under the headline, "San Joseans Strike It Rich Near Nome, Alaska."

French wrote, "The Government records show that more gold has been taken out of the Seward Purchase than from any one section on the face of the globe in the same time . . ."[8] For the summer of 1900 alone, French estimated that $7,000,000 of gold was mined. Commercial gold mines still work the Seward Peninsula interior, and a few miners still rock the beach sand each summer.

SEVERAL photographers set up gold rush studios in Nome, but Will may have been the only Sourdough who was also an accomplished photographer. He lugged his cumbersome, twenty-pound view camera with him wherever he went, and he photographed every aspect of his life as a Sourdough—sea travel, mining operations, city life in Nome, dog sledding, storms and blizzards, landscape, leisure, and his native neighbors.

While Will's photographs show what can't be told, his letters to his parents and his sister tell what can't be shown. He hand delivered these letters to steamships about to leave for California. His writing, like his photographs, is simple and beautiful, revealing the details of his life in Alaska as well as the life he left behind in California. Ed did not write as often as Will, but his letters—frank, brief, vivid—often say what his brother left unsaid.

Now the brothers describe their remarkable journey in their own words and images.

—Editor

NOTES

1. L.H. French, *Nome Nuggets 1901*. Northwest Publishing Co., 1983. From the foreword by T. Cole, p. 7.
2. Ibid., p. 31.
3. Ibid.
4. Ibid.
5. George Bird Grinnell, *Alaska 1899, Essays from the Harriman Expedition*. University of Washington Press, 1995, p. 183.
6. French, *Nome Nuggets*, p. 23.
7. Ibid., p. 21.
8. Ibid., p. 47.

Caution!

TO THOSE who contemplate going to Alaska, to battle with the climate, to cross almost impassable country, to ford streams nearly as cold in the summer as they are during the long Arctic winters, I would say, "don't."

Gold is there in untold quantities, though it is not for the average man; and when such a one stumbles upon it, as such sometimes do, it is by the merest chance.

The gold seeker in Alaska should be a man of iron nerve and constitution.

He should, by all means, possess some practical knowledge of gold-mining.

He should have an objective point, about which he must obtain all the accurate information possible before starting.

He should be supplied with a perfect outfit, or equipment, for the season in the far north.

He should have money to carry out his cherished plans.

He must either purchase claims, or interests in claims, or wander far from the present mining districts, on long and costly prospecting tours to obtain anything of value.

The thousands who return from the Nome regions, condemning the country, are like the hundreds and thousands who have returned from every gold rush. Many of the disappointed arrived on the gold fields without a dollar in their pockets or a penny's worth of supplies, with the mad idea that they would be able to wash out gold enough, during their first day on shore, to purchase the much needed dinner.

They returned from California in the early fifties, denouncing the country and all who remained in it. They did the same from the Comstock and Bodie regions later; and, still later, from Leadville and Cripple Creek. Yet all these regions have yielded millions. In Australia and South Africa, the story has been the same.

The human failure is loud in his denunciation of everything and everybody.

—Written in 1901 by L. H. French, manager of the
Cape Nome Hydraulic Mining Company
from *Nome Nuggets*

show to morrow, also a funeral to morrow "Sat" also base ball + a fight or two to kill time with. The harbor is full of ships + they have a great time coaling. It is very cold here + those chest protectors are just the thing. Boat builders are doing a rushing business. Talk about tin horn gamblers & men with guns, we have plenty. We have two men in irons on this ship who tried to kill each other with pistols, but they were not good shots. Also two of our ladies of which we have 50 got into a drunken row and thought that the other must die pulled their guns,

California Ranch
"Orchards in full bloom.."

The McDaniel family ranch, along today's Naglee Street in San Jose, circa 1890. The center portion of the house, with a simple gabled roof and a chimney, was the original ranch house. The portion at right, with shorter windows and an encircling porch, was a later addition.

Above: Will and Ed McDaniel and a neighbor boy gather hay on the ranch in San Jose, circa 1896.

Opposite, top: Josiah and Amanda McDaniel, parents of Will and Ed. Opposite, bottom left: Lulu McDaniel, younger sister of Will and Ed. Many of the letters were addressed to her. Opposite, bottom right: Ed and Will pose with two neighbor girls and Lulu, all dressed for roles in amateur theatricals, circa 1895.

The steamship St. Paul *prepares for departure from San Francisco for Nome, Alaska, 1902.*

Sea Legs
"We were packed in the hold like cattle."

San Francisco, June 9, 1899

Dear Folks,

    Went aboard the Steamer *Bertha* at 3:30 p.m. She pulled out into the stream and pointed her nose for the Heads. I went down to supper at 5:30 p.m. Was feeling fine. As I was sitting at the table I began to get dizzy. I ate a big supper and came on deck and gave it to the fish. I went to my stateroom and got into my bunk. There I lay for 4 days and nights, could not eat anything, but drank water and sucked limes. I bought 25 cents worth—4 dozen. I just had to take it—lost about 20 lbs.

    I had 3 bad dreams last Monday night. The first was that one of the crew came and threw me overboard, and I never made a move but felt fine when I was sinking in the water. Second dream was I had a sugar pine board 2 ft. by 12 inches inside of me and they were stretching my stomach over it. The next dream was that someone had my stomach twisted up like you would twist up a dishrag to get the water out of it. So you can see what seasickness is.

    This is Thursday, nearly one week since we left home, but it seems like 2 months. Nothing but the sea to see and 14 "goonies", sea birds which have followed us from Frisco. We are alone on the sea 1000 miles from land. If anything should happen, I think we would be cooked.

—Your son, E.J.M.

EDITOR'S NOTE: The McDaniel brothers made several trips on different ships between California and Alaska. The photographs and the letters in this section are from various voyages in different years.

"Dropping the Pilot": the Harbor Pilot leads the S.S. Zealandia *out through the Golden Gate.*

"We were just packed in the hold like cattle. Most of the steerage were foreigners and dirty as hogs. When they were seasick they just vomited on the floor, and spitting and expectorating made the condition of things frightful." —Will, S.S. Zealandia, June 15, 1900.

Storm in mid-ocean: a view from the steamship Roanoke *in the North Pacific, November, 1901.*

Mid-ocean, May 28, 1900

Dear Sister,

    Well, here we are over a thousand miles out on the Pacific. We had a great time getting off last Monday. Of all the jams you ever saw, that was the worst. I got on board about 20 minutes before we sailed and thought I would be smashed flat. We left the dock and anchored off Black Point where the tickets were collected and everybody rounded up. One stowaway was sent back on the tug and we were off. We were all feeling fine for the first 10 or 15 miles, then Ed was the first to grow sick. I held off to the last but got it in the neck too.

    Thursday we were struck by a Sou'wester and then the fun began. I just wish mama could have been on board for just one minute. The sea came up in great style and the wind blew about 40 miles an hour. Well, the old *Zealandia* just rolled like a pig in a hog wallow. Ed and I were on deck but when her sail went under, we got below. The seas came over her bow and down the decks two feet deep. Next morning while Ed was above, a life line gave and 3 or 4 men were hurt. Ed went down and got soaked. I went up on the hurricane deck with the Kodak and managed to get two snaps. Hope they are good. Ed said this was worse than his trip last fall. Ed says I look like I had lost 25 pounds and I guess I have if feelings count.

    —Wilfred, *S.S. Zealandia*

Returning to California on the hurricane deck of the steamship Senator, *November 1900. "The grub is as follows. Breakfast: Mush—very poor, with lumps as big as an egg in it, boiled potatoes and fried meat and belly wash coffee. Dinner: Boiled potatoes. Mush is left out and stew substituted. Supper: Just read the dinner menu backwards and you have it."* —Will

Mid-ocean, May 28, 1900

Dear Folks,

    We all have our sea legs now and are enjoying ourselves more. Yesterday we had preaching and singing up on the hurricane deck, a preacher named Meserve from Oakland. During the service the preacher said he wanted no collection taken and would not have it. At the evening service, one of the waiters went through the crowd and got quite a sum which he made a sneak with. But they fixed him all right. The officers shackled him to the brace rods upon the hurricane deck for 3 hours in the cold and then put him down in the coal hold. He is the second of the crew to be in irons.

    I suppose you want to know something of our surroundings. Well, the Z. is a pretty big boat. If you could put her on Naglee street, she would lack just 22 feet from reaching our place. She is about 40 feet wide and draws 23 feet of water, very narrow, which makes her a great roller. Now for the steerage. There are about 450 in the hold. All nationalities and all classes. We have canvas bunks to sleep on, built 2 wide and 3 high, with a narrow passage between.

    The grub is as follows. Breakfast: Mush—very poor with lumps as big as an egg in it, boiled potatoes and fried meat and belly wash coffee. Dinner: Boiled potatoes. Mush is left out and stew substituted. Supper: Just read the dinner menu backwards and you have it. As yesterday was Sunday, we had pickles.

    I have written this letter while standing on one foot leaning against a bunk, and an old oil light bobbing over me so don't criticize.

—Wilfred

Opposite:
Steamship Roanoke,
Captain Weaver, Master.
North Pacific, 1903.

Seattle stopover, June 1901.

Steamship Oregon *at Pier 4, Seattle.*

Steamer *St. Paul*
Lat. 53 N, Long. 160 W
June 16, 1901

Dear Parents,

    Well, here we are, about 130 miles from Unalaska, and just two weeks from home. When we reach there we shall have traveled 2750 miles with 800 more to go. The sea has been like a pond all the way. We had our sea legs by the time we got to Seattle so that we have enjoyed the trip from there to Dutch Harbor. We have fine food all the time. We had strawberries at breakfast yesterday and roast goose for dinner, twice. I had to turn my goose loose at 1:00 a.m. the last time I ate it. Our room is now heated by steam as the weather is getting colder. There was a concert in the saloon a few evenings ago and I hear there will be another this eve.

    The big U.S. transport *Warren* started from Seattle a few hours after our boat, bound for Nome. She overtook us and passed us in the evening. We cold see her masts for a day, then for two days could see her smoke, then she disappeared.

    I have had one case of extraction so far, but sorry to say the patient was busted so did not get anything except the experience and a chance to try my new forcep.*

        —With love, Will

*Will was an amateur dentist.

Traveling second class: Ed writes in his diary aboard the St. Paul, *1903.*

Dutch Harbor on Unalaska Island in the Aleutian Archipelago, 1900. "This is a very beautiful harbor, formed by the islands. The water is calm as a pond but is quite deep." —Will

Dutch Harbor

"Hurray! Land in sight!"

Unalaska, Thursday, June 22, 1899

Dear Folks,

    I suppose you want to know how I am getting along, whether I am dead or alive. We arrived at Dutch Harbor yesterday. We have stopped here for coal and water. I helped shovel coal last night to 10 o'clock just to get some exercise, and I felt much better. It is a land-locked place among the islands, a mountainous country of solid rock, and the peaks are covered with snow. The town is not much of a place, about 200 people and mostly natives, that is, half breeds, partly Russian and Indian. The people are all short, under 5 ft., heavy.

    The *Homer*, which left Frisco 3 days before we did, arrived yesterday at Dutch Harbor too. She is loaded down beyond what the law requires and carried 146 passengers. The captain of our boat said that she was nothing but a coffin for the people if they should happen to get into a storm. There is a rumor here that the *National City,* an old steamer which comes up here, is lost with all hands. We don't know how true the rumor is. So you see it pays to go on a good boat. You have no idea how the sea is. It is as smooth as the water at Alviso one day and the next it is rolling mountains high, which look like they would tear the ship to pieces. It is not pleasant to have the ship roll over sideways so that her lower deck nearly comes to the water. We had a great time eating our meals when she would roll. We would let everything go and grab our coffee and drink it so as to keep it. The rest of the things, dishes and grub, would slide back and forth on the table. So you can see what a sea voyage is. I would rather make mine in a land schooner any day. Love to all and friends,

—Yours, E.J.M.

"We came into Dutch Harbor making 17 miles per hour. The Zealandia is the largest boat and the fastest; she is a good sea boat but a bad roller. During the gale her decks were under water all the time. There are 25 boats in the harbor." —Will, June 2, 1900.

View of the village of Unalaska from Dutch Harbor, with the Russian Orthodox church at center.

St. Michaels,
Wednesday, June 28, 1899

Dear Folks,

The city here is composed of 3 separate towns, 3 different companies, and they each have their land barbed wired off. I went through the native village and found queer looking houses made of mud.

They bury their dead right back of their houses on top of the ground. They put the dead in an old box on top of the ground, then they drive four stakes around the box and pile some driftwood on top. Next they hang his best bow and arrow on one of the stakes, and on the 3 other stakes hang his best dog whip and paddles. They also pile his canoe and dog sled on top of the wood. Some of the boxes have fallen to pieces and parts of the skeleton are lying around the heap. I saw one grave where some of the small bones were lying scattered around, and the skull on the outside, with particles of hair on it, grinning at you.

I have seen some fine walrus tusks which had figures worked on them. The natives used the nicotine out of their pipes for the black outlines, and for the coloring they used colored cloth which they boil and color it in some way. If I get rich you will see some of their work.

I have seen no mosquitoes yet. Oh, if I only had some ripe apricots and apples to eat. Write to me and tell me all the news. Love to all,

—Your son, E.J. McDaniel

Aleut house, or Barabara, in Unalaska.

Dutch Harbor, Alaska,
June 4, 1900

Dear Folks,

 We are both laid up with bad colds so that we do not feel much like writing or doing anything else. Last Friday Ed and I took an 8 mile walk, partly around the island. We found an oil can and had a mussel dinner. We enjoyed it more than anything we have had. The weather has been cloudy and chilly. Everything is white with snow except around the beach. This is a very beautiful harbor, formed by the islands. The water is calm as a pond but is quite deep.

 There are a lot of characters on board, both men and women. Tin horn gamblers and thieves. Had a shooting scrape the other night. No one was hurt and the shooter was ironed and placed on the U.S. gun boat *Wheeling*. He'll not get to Nome for a while, I guess.

 We all vow we'll never get caught in the steerage again. The crowd we are forced to be with is a dirty lot. When a fellow is sick and has nothing to listen to but their jabbering, yelling, and profanity, it nearly drives one crazy. I think about half of them are anarchists and socialists. They will strike the wrong thing if they do as they think and talk when they get to Nome. One would think from the way some talk they are just going to kill every man they take a notion to.

 If you saw the report that we hear is in the states, that the *Zealandia* is lost, I suppose you have us all dead and buried. Love to all,

 —Wilfred

Aleut woman and child, Unalaska.

Dutch Harbor, Alaska,
June 6, 1900

Dear Mother,

News is rather scarce here and it's hard to think of anything to write about.

Ed and I attended services at the Russian Cathedral at Unalaska last Saturday. For about an hour before the doors opened, the bells were jangling out some very odd, but not discordant, music. All the devotees stood at the door, the men all on one side, and the women and children on the other. The members are all Aleuts and Russian, and they looked very picturesque in their bright colored dress.

When the door was opened everybody went in, the men on one side and the women on the other, and everybody stands as there are no seats in the church. They have a choir composed of Aleut boys. I wish you could have heard the singing. The priest went through some mummery in Russian and the chimes came in at opportune times during the ceremony. After a while a priest came out holding a golden cross which everyone kissed, and later, the crowd passed in front of the priest and kissed his hand. After the kissing was over, the service was over. The church is gorgeous inside, all covered with pictures and images and lighted with candles. All the decorations are green and red, making it very showy.

The other day we took a long tramp to the top of a peak near the bay. The other side of the peak rises almost perpendicular from the Bering Sea and is nothing but rocky cliffs and precipices from top to bottom. Took several pictures while on top.

—With love to all, Wilfred

Will and Ed at the summit of a peak on Amaknak Island, near Dutch Harbor.

Dutch Harbor, June 7, 1900

Dear Folks,

We are still at port with no prospect of getting any farther north. One steam schooner arrived in port this morning which tried to get to Nome but had to get back. Four boats are up there now frozen in. The *Bear* is up there now trying to get some of the ships out. The *Catherine Sudden* came near being sunk by the ice. She had her bows stove in. The captain has issued an order to all ships' masters in the harbor not to proceed north till the middle of next week.

Talk about a crowd—we have it here. Every boat that has left the States for Alaska is here in the harbor. All kinds of people here. Every kind of gambling games. We have a steam laundry and plenty of saloons, also millions of phonographs. The people are crazy here for anything. They will break their necks to see a fight or a boat come in. We have baseball between the different ships which helps to pass the time away. We will have a variety show tomorrow—also a funeral.

Talk about tin horn gamblers and men with guns, we have plenty. We have two men in irons on this ship who tried to kill each other with pistols, but they were not good shots. Also two of our ladies, of which we have 50, got into a drunken row and thought that the other must die, pulled their guns on each other, but were separated and put in the hold of the ship with the other fellows.

You ought to see the stores of which there are two. They are all sold out and no way of getting anything more. The people here are coining money. Boatmen who ferry from ship to ship are making $25 to $50 per day. About 50 ships in the harbor now. Among them is the gunboat *Wheeling* and revenue cutter *Rush*. They had the Marines to guard natives who are loading the ships with coal. We had a strike among them and whites over wages.

I would like to have some fruit pretty bad.

—Love to all, E.J.M.

Children from the Jesse Lee Home, a Methodist orphanage at Dutch Harbor.

                        June 20, 1901, Steamer *St. Paul*

Sunday night all the *St. Paul's* passengers who did not go to the saloons and gambling places here went down to the Jesse Lee Home to a sacred song service. The crowd sang for about an hour, Eskimos and all. There are about 30 Aleut and Eskimo children at the home. It is an orphans' home for these native children.   —Will

View from the S.S. Zealandia, Bering Sea, June 1900.

Through the Ice Floes
"Four Ships are Frozen In . . . "

June 9, 1900

Dear Folks,

Finshed taking coal at 10 a.m. and are preparing to leave. Left the wharf at 11 a.m. The tug *Meteor* pulled us around and then we were off. We had a grand farewell. Every steamer blew us a salute of three long blasts. These were answered individually by the *Zealandia*. Passed an active volcano on our starboard about 1 p.m.

June 11, 1900

The sun is out part of the time and then it fogs up again. The rigging is covered with ice and frost. We are out of the floes and among the broken cakes and bergs. We are barely moving and winding in and out among the ice blocks. We are now pushing our way, now backing and turning. When the ship strikes the ice she trembles from stem to stern.

June 12, 1900

We are getting into larger icebergs as we go north. The ice is whiter and more solid. Passed many ice blocks that stood 10 ft. above water and 200 ft. across. Some of them are very beautiful, all sorts of fantastic shapes and forms. We get some great shakes when the old boat strikes the ice. Worse than an earthquake. Today makes 22 days from S.F.

—Will

Thursday, June 20, 1901
Steamer *St. Paul*

Dear Lulu,

We left Unalaska and ran into ice the next day at noon. The ice is 200 miles further south this year than it has been for several years. We started into the ice, trying to get next to shore, but the captain thought it risky so turned around and took a S.W. course for the Pribiloff Isls. The captain expected to go toward Siberia and keep outside the ice but we met the S.S. *Homer* coming back from our intended course. She ran up alongside and reported. Said she had been 21 days trying to get through but could not get nearer than 25 miles to St. Lawrence Is. as the sea was solid ice. We lost 24 hours and went 200 miles for nothing. We turned around and retraced our course - went through the ice floes and got in open sea yesterday. See some big icebergs, but no floes. Some of them are as big as the *St. Paul*.

We have had a very pleasant trip all the way, and could not ask for a smoother sea. We took on a boat load of fresh mackerel at Unalaska. They are splendid. We also have fresh codfish. These fish are all caught among the islands. Saw many fine furs at Unalaska and they are very cheap now. Sealskins $4 to $6, fox — red $2 & $3, white fox $2.50 to $6.

—With love, Wilfred

S.S. St. Paul *entering the Bering Sea, Captain Hayes, Master. June 1903.*

S.S. Zealandia *bucking ice in the Bering Sea, June 1900. Captain Dowdell, Master. "We have now been in the ice four days. Everyone is uneasy and hoping for clear sea."*

Right: S.S. St. Paul *in Bering Sea ice, 1903. "If a gale should come up while we are in the ice . . we would go to the bottom, as the ice would crush our boat like an eggshell"*

Night on the Bering Sea, near the Pribiloff Islands: S.S. St. Paul, 1903. "We are out of the floes and among the cakes and bergs. We are barely moving, and winding in and out among the ice blocks." —Will

June 22, 1901

Dear Folks,

 Ship's log as follows:

  Thermometer registers 42 degrees. Time is 9:05.
  Anchored in 15 fathoms water 5 miles off Nunivak Island
  400 miles from Dutch Harbor.
  167 West Longitude, 60 North Latitude.
  Grounded in mud flats 7 p.m., June 22, 1901.
  Ship running half speed. Grounded full length.
  Reversed engines at full speed and got off.
  Stuck in 3 fathoms of water. Ship draws 3 1/6 fathoms.
  Off our course on account of heavy fog and ice.
  No panic among passengers.
  Officers all at their post.
  Ship rocked from port to starboard after striking.

 We are now anchored in 15 fathoms of water for the night or until the heavy weather clears. Ship's doctor busy with broken heads caused by too much whiskey.

 Captain has been on the bridge all week. Has not had his clothes off, has all meals sent up to him. He has had to stand a great deal of abuse but he has had the worst weather known for years in these latitudes.

 We will soon be dumped off like a lot of cattle on the cold bleak coast of Nome. We will be left to scratch as best we can.

       —Yours, E.J. McDaniel

S.S. Victoria *in the Bering Strait.*

S.S. Zealandia *arrives in Nome anchorage, June 1900.* "We will soon be dumped off like a lot of cattle on the cold, bleak coast of Nome." —Ed

Nome, the New Frontier
"Read all about the bloody murder!"

Nome, June 15, 1900

Dear Folks,

Here we are at last, putting into the anchorage at Nome. It is now 4 a.m. The *Zealandia* makes the 20th vessel in the harbor. As far as one can see the beach is covered with tents. It is a dreary looking place. Hills are covered with snow. Mining is going on all along the beach.

We will never go steerage again. Now that our miserable trip is over, and you can't worry about us, I'll tell you about it. We were just packed in the hold like cattle. Most of the steerage were foreigners and dirty as hogs. When they were seasick they just vomited on the floor. The ship's company did not seem to care whether we landed alive or dead. Just imagine the condition of that boat with 400 men in one place after 2 or 3 weeks. It was only the cold climate that kept down a pestilence. There were 3 or 4 cases of pneumonia. One poor fellow died. An hour before he died, the doctor had the smoking room fitted up as a hospital and had the man taken from the hold, but it was too late.

Our food was very poor and coarse. Our coffee was made of navy beans and carrots. Had dishwater soup for dinner and cold boiled soggy potatoes 3 times a day. For supper we had a foul concoction called mulligan stew. It was impossible to get much sleep as gambling was going on and sick men were coughing and cursing, and I tell you one could imagine oneself in the lower region while sick, bad enough for a well man.

We are now getting located and got our freight. There are about 20,000 people at Cape Nome and in this vicinity. If our pictures are good you will see some novel sights.

—Love to all, Wilfred

The Anvil Railroad ran from Nome out the pier to the loading dock.

Cape Nome Beach, June 18, 1900

Well, we are here on the beach among thousands of others in the same fix. We do not know what we are going to do. They have not started to work on the creeks yet as they are not thawed out, that is, the ground.

Nome City is composed of tents and buildings. Wages are high—$1.00 per hour for common labor. If I was well we would go to work at building, $1.50 per hour, as there is plenty of work.

—Love to all, Wilfred

Nome, 1900: "Just imagine 25 miles of beach covered with tents and people." —Will

Nome, June 22, 1901

We arrived at Nome anchorage this evening at 6 o'clock. The beach looks desolate where we worked last year. It is covered with snow. We cannot see our cabin yet—we look for it with glasses. We can see quite an improvement in the town, quite a few new buildings. The doctor from town came out to inspect the ship and he said that 2000 people wintered there and the health of the camp was never better. Hardly any sickness at all.

—Yours, E.J. McDaniel

Nome, along the Snake River: "Everything here is for sale. All kinds of business and property. Outfits are selling very cheaply." —Will

Nome City, July 2, 1900

Dear Folks,

    We moved our camp day before yesterday about 8 miles north of where we first camped. We are now on the ground where we expect our freight to be landed. We had to make two trips with our boat. We were getting very crowded where we were. Hardly room to get between the tents. Just imagine 25 miles of beach covered with tents and people. We are now in a fine place. Plenty of room and lots of wood.

    The town of Nome is going to be a pest hole and we are all glad to get away from it. The town is all one street which is about 5 miles long. The street is crowded with a surging mass of humanity all of the time. There have been about 5 men shot and killed since we arrived. The town is under military law and the soldiers are doing police duty. The tough element are all in town so that we will not see anything of them.

    We have 2 or 3 papers published here. Newsboys go down the street shouting, "Gold-digger here! Read all about the bloody murder! Only 25 cents!"

    Very little money is being spent here as far as I can tell. There are lots of lunch counters and restaurants and all sorts of places, but they don't seem to do much business as people won't spend their money until they make some. There is a dairy here too. Milk sells for 50 cents a qt., sugar 5 lbs. for $1.00, spuds 4 to 5 cents a lb., flour $2.50 to $3.50 a sack, bacon 25 cents a lb., beans 10 cents a lb.

    We are getting hardened to work now. When we first landed we could not do anything at all. I have a rock from an old grave at the Russian Church at Dutch Harbor for Edith Hall.

    I must close as I have run down.

—Wilfred

Nome: A wooden sidewalk lines the street in front of the Occidental Hotel, while citizens bask in the sun on a day of rest. The hotel is very similar to buildings put up in San Francisco at the turn of the century.

Second Street in Nome is becoming civilized: two hotels—the Royal and the more imposing Lawrence—offer accommodations, while the façade of the grocery store, still under construction, boasts decorative shingle work in the latest style. The planked street is an enormous improvement over mud. "Five men have been shot and killed since we arrived. The town is under military law and the soldiers are doing police duty." —Will

The Anvil Lodge, Nome, was a building of considerable architectural refinement, with crested gables, a bracketed cornice, and quoins decorating all the outer corners—a lavish structure, considering that all building materials had to be imported at great expense.

The fire of 1905 destroyed dozens of buildings in Nome. "The fire did a great deal of damage. It burned out the saloon and tenderloin district, besides restaurants, stores and shops. The carpenters were busy rebuilding as fast as they could get lumber."
—Will

The cemetery at Nome: "We have two or three papers published here. Newsboys go down the street shouting 'Gold Digger here! Read all about the bloody murder! Only 25 cents!'" —Will

A paddlewheel river boat rests on the Snake River at Nome, 1903.

Nome, September 19, 1905

We went down to Nome last Friday with the boat and got one ton of groceries. Got our winter's supply of milk and sugar. Got 5 cases of Carnations Cream and 150 lbs. of sugar, also 200 lbs of flour, 250 of spuds, ham, and bacon. Had a hard trip. Ed did not feel well and I had to manage the towline both ways. That's a hard way to save money, but we saved 10 or 12 dollars anyway.

—Wilfred

Snowing at Nome, June 16, 1910. One of Will's friends evidently sent him this negative, since Will's last trip to Nome was in 1908.

Unloading mining equipment at a new claim near Cripple River. "We have staked a beach claim 50 feet x 690 feet. It is called Umooluktuk claim." —Will

Mining
"I can see gold all through the sand!"

Council City, Alaska, Saturday, July 21, 1899

Dear Will,

I am well and having a pretty good time. We have been working on the Sweet Cake claim, Number One above discovery. The claim is no good, but the one below us is pretty good. That is the one the boys got their money out of last year. They say that they have taken this spring about $3200. You don't want to believe all the yarns in Alaska. I have seen no gold dust or any good prospects yet and would not trade the Trinity mine for all the Alaska mines.

It is awfully hard to live up here. The mosquitoes are thick as bees and it rains all the time and the sun never sets. The ground is covered with moss and water. As you walk one foot goes out of sight and you are on your back. This country is not what it is cracked up to be. We are all well and you might say happy if we had gold.

Well, I must close as I can't stand the mosquitoes any longer.

July 30, 1899

Alaska is a hard place to live in. If there is no money up here for me I will get out of here this fall. The country is staked all around and of no earthly account.

It is very hot this week, from 90 to 100 degrees. I have been swimming in the river. They say we are 1500 miles from the north pole. We can see volcanoes smoking around us.

You ought to see my whiskers. They are fine for mosquitoes. I wish I had some green fruit.

—Yours truly, E. J. McD.

EDITOR'S NOTE: Ed McDaniel went to Alaska alone in 1899, and here is writing to his brother Wilfred in San Jose.

St. Michaels, Alaska, September 21, 1899

Dear Will,

    Well here I am on my way home at last. We are getting out of the country none too fast as it is beginning to freeze up the river, 12 inches of ice floating in the water. Mr. King sold out his interest in his mines. He treated us very badly in the deal. We opened up the mine on Sweet Cake and he goes and sells us out. I have over $200 in gold dust. Some nice nuggets I will keep. If I had known how things were going to turn out this season, I would now have over a $1000 by going to Nome. But King wanted me to stay and develop the property as he thinks I am a great miner and that is what I get.

    There are lots of men here who are destitute—the government will have to take them out of the country. It is a hard life up here and a man is lucky that gets out with his health or life. The chances we take are great but if I come back here I will know the ropes.

    Fifteen of us Sweet Cake boys are going to sail from here, St. Michaels on the *Louise B. Kennie* for San Francisco—fare $60. It is our only chance to get out of the country. The steamers are engaged ahead and have more than they can carry. The *Kennie* is a two masted schooner. She is a new vessel and a fast sailor. I have some ivories that I got from the natives. I am a hard-looking traveler with whiskers and old clothes. I wear mukluks, a native boot made out of seal. This country would be a fine place if the seasons were longer, but as it is, you can only count on 90 days. I have been sleeping on frozen ground all summer and have seen the thermometer 100 degrees in the shade. Love to all and hope I will make a safe voyage.

    —Yours, E.J. McDaniel

Ed and Jessie on their beach claim. Sea water was pumped through sluice boxes, and beach sand was shoveled into the running water. Gold, heavier than the sand, was collected in riffles on the bottom of the sluice box.

"We have three good men hired. We have a Mr. Hughes, who is foreman when we are not around, and it saves us a great deal of worry to have someone we can leave in charge." —Will

Working the claim, 1903. "We have a male quartet in our camp. We sing everything we know and have some pretty good music."
—*Will*

July 19, 1900

Dear Folks,

We got to sluicing last Sunday and made a 50 hour run. We hired 2 men and I ran the night shift. We cleaned up $90. We discharged the men as they were not shovelers and did not know how to work. I am writing this while cooking breakfast, so excuse the appearance. Breakfast is ready.

Had mush, fried rice, hot biscuits, syrup and coffee. Feel ready for work now. We are away from town and glad of it. Don't want to go there. It's full of bums and sure thing men. Lots of men are getting in bad circumstances here. I think the government will have to take them out.

I have been home visiting in my dreams 4 times. I wonder what that means anyway. We get mail all right. One of mama's letters was 33 days in reaching us.

—With love to all, Will

Cape Nome, Alaska, July 22, 1900

Dear Folks,

Ed and I are both in fine health and doing well. You may hear of the accident before you get this. Rouse lost his life by being tangled in the rope on the gipsy of the engine. Ed and I have been afraid of the thing and have never touched it, but Rouse said he had been in the business for 4 or 5 years and thought he understood it. He and Ed were pulling up the oil barrels from the beach and had all but two up when the rope slipped and began whirling and twisting. The rope got a twist around his leg and drew him over the gipsy and whirled him around three or four times until the momentum of the engine ceased. When we got him out his leg fell off, cut clean off at the knee. Rouse did not know his leg was gone until he saw it and asked, "What's that?" Then he realized what had happened and collapsed. We had him in a cabin and Mr. Tenney, the doctor, Ed and I and two other men were with him when he died. I feel very sorry for his folks.

They objected to his coming, too. We were just getting started in good shape and making some money.

Now do not worry over us. We have never touched that gipsy and you may know that we never will.

—Love to all, Wilfred

Ed with a pan of gold amalgam—gold flecks held together with mercury (quicksilver) to form lumps. Edwards Creek Claim.

Nome, Alaska, August 2, 1900

Dear Folks,

Well, here we are tied up on the golden beach of Alaska. We had papers served on us this morning prohibiting us from working, moving our plant or sluice boxes. Everything on the beach is in a great mix-up. All the plants are shut down and awaiting developments. There have been lots of arrests made and the Commissioner has decided against the miners who have been bound over to appear before the District Court. It's a shame and an outrage that the thing has gone as it has. There are some 200 plants in operation here on the beach. We were doing well and would make a good little pile if we could work.

August. 3, 1900

The owners of the tundra claim served a notice on us. We went down and talked with the head man of the company and he wants us to stay and work. He wants $500 for a two month lease. We are in a quandry. We are well located and are just fairly started; if we leave, we can't do anything more and if we stay we will have to lease the property. We are going to see him today and try and get a cheaper lease. It's too much for what we get out.

There is lots of fun here staking claims. We have staked a beach claim 50 ft. x 690 ft. It is called the Umooluktuk claim. The claims here are in a terrible muddle, from 2 to 4 claimants to every claim.

We looked for mail on the last boat but got none. Give our best wishes to all.

—With love, Will

Rouse and Ed, shoveling.

"We are among the few successful miners here, and we owe it to our experience with engines and pumps and our experience in California mining." —Will, August 1900.

Indian Village, Nome, August 18, 1901

Dear Folks,

    We have spent as far as our books show $1227.92 in cash since the 1st of June. What do you think of that?—all that money we have made ourselves in a short time. You can think what a pleasure it is to handle it even if we can't keep it. We have spent more than that counting the discount on gold dust by selling it at $16 per oz. when it is worth $17.50. We now have $500 lying around the cabin, part in a pair of old shoes, $400 in 3 gold pans, $25 or $30 in an old tea can and the Lord knows where the rest is scattered.

    We all well fixed in Alaska, in fact better than most people. We are probably worth $2,000 in Alaska property, that is if we could get a fair price for our belongings. I eat like a pig-- 1 hour after eating I could eat another big feed. Well, I must close.

—E.J.M.

Nome, Alaska, August 18, 1901

Dear Folks,

    Well, here it is Sunday again and one week less for the miners. We have been working all day making some new boxes and fixing up the engine. We have now worked about 250 ft. of beach, as much as we did all of last season. We are disappointed in not getting the cleanups we got last year, although our last two look much better than the former one. The paying claims are nearly all in the court and forty claimants for each. When a good claim is opened, then the racket begins. You generally lose either way. If you strike it then you're stopped by litigation, and if you don't strike it, you stop anyway.

    I suppose you spend your Sundays as usual, church and board meetings and late dinners? While you folks were all togged up in your good clothes today listening to Rev. Herrold, I was sitting in the engine tent inside a pair of old greasy overalls filing the cross head brasses and keeping time to "How Firm A Foundation," grease and smut all over me, quite a contrast to white collars and cuffs and a seat in the choir, eh? I would just like to put Rev. H. through a few days of Cape Nome life. I think he would be willing to quit very soon.

—Wilfred

Gold amalgam, after heating in a retort to remove mercury: 95 ounces, with a value of $3,250.

Gold amalgam: $800 in eight days. "We get up at 5:30 and cook and eat and then I get the engine and pump ready at 6:30. By the time supper is over it is bed time. Daylight lasts from 3 a.m. till about 10:30 p.m."
—Will

September 16, 1901

Dear Papa,

    As I was going downtown today to get $300 to pay the men, I thought I would send a letter out. The fleet of vessels is in again. They will make another trip, I suppose, and that will be the last. This month has been the finest of the season. Have not lost a day of work to weather since the 8th of July. We have had one Sunday off.

    We have 3 men hired all the time and have worked 400 ft. of ground wide and 130 ft. in length of boxes so you can see the amount of dirt handled. It averages over 4 ft. in depth. We have taken out $3,000 in gold. We have saved up for ourselves, outside of our own expense, about $1,500 as near as I can get at it. We would have taken out more, but just as it always is, when the season is closing we strike good ground. We are working old ground but find the pay down in bedrock. We think we can run till the last of October. I am going to buy some pistols today to protect ourselves. Hope you are all well. We are in fine health. I will close. Love to all.

—E.J. McDaniel

September 4, 1902

Dear Folks,

    Poor Dutch John has come to grief. After he and the young fellow, Albert, left us, they went partners and worked about 100 yards from our cabin. Albert soon got tired of his partner and they had trouble and separated, but neither moved away—just went it alone. Three days ago Albert came over to get a tool and talked for half an hour. When he returned to his tent, he found his money gone, 140 dollars. He asked John if he had seen anyone around and he said no so he had John arrested and he is now in jail to be tried Sept. 15th. Bail is $1,000 so he stays in jail.

    If we can get good ground and run late, we will take out as much as last year. We work pretty hard to get it and think we earn it all. I am busy from 6:30 a.m. til 7 and 8 p.m. At night one feels like just letting everything go to pieces, but in the morning we go at it with renewed energy and put the sand through. A mortgage is a very heavy thing to lift. I estimate ours has weighed so far, about 20,000 tons of sand in two years. Ah len a moot (goodbye)

—Will

On their claim near Edwards Creek the McDaniel brothers used a steam thawer to melt permafrost so that they could retrieve and sluice sand from ancient beach lines.

"After being lowered in the bucket . . . I filled the bucket with sand and gravel, and Ed hoisted it and dumped it. Ed shouted down the shaft, 'I just scooped up a handful of black sand and I can see gold all through it.'" —Will

Thawing the Tundra

The "burning down" method of prospecting was slow and laborious; drift wood from the beach was hauled to the claim, a fire built on the selected spot and kept burning for several hours. The few inches of tundra thus thawed would be removed and another fire built. From four to six inches a day was the usual depth gained. Weeks, and even months were consumed in sinking a shaft to the bedrock, a distance varying from twenty to thirty feet. The frozen sand and gravel resisted all efforts made by the pick, merely blunting the tool on its concrete-like surface. Occasional layers of ice and frozen muck had to be removed with a pick, as the water from the melted ice would extinguish the fire, putting an end to any further thawing from that source.

This deposit of sand and gravel was an ancient sea formation, evidently an old beach formed by the Bering Sea during a remote age, the up-lift of land causing the sea to recede to its present level. This "second beach line" was traced for many miles along the coast in the vicinity of Nome, and in many localities considerable gold was mined; layers of black and ruby sand were found containing gold in varying quantities.

In the sands of the ancient beach, later removed from the tunnels and drifts by steam thawing, many fossils were found. At one point, close to the clay bottom, a huge bone, the size of a man's body, was uncovered. Buried in the sand during ages past, the sea had deposited layers of gold-bearing black and ruby sand both under and above the huge fossil. From the size and shape of the fossil, and its porous structure, we decided that it was the lower jaw bone of a prehistoric whale, the character of bone being the same as that of similar bones found on the sea shore.

It was after 9 a.m. before the tardy sun gave us light enough to continue our work. The smoke-stack, with guy wires attached to anchor it securely against the winter gales, was raised and placed in position. Stakes were set in

Editor's note: Wilfred McDaniel wrote a memoir, entitled "Alaska Beckons," in 1946. This narrative is an excerpt from that work.

Prospecting on the sub-marine beach line. The thawed and excavated sand was piled up to wait for warmer weather, when water was available for sluicing.

holes dug in the frozen ground, firmly secured by pouring a bucket of water around them, the quickly-formed ice holding as solidly as concrete.

A windlass was built and located over the shaft for hoisting the thawed sand and gravel, and also, to lower and raise the one engaged in setting the thawing points or removing the material from the drifts. After being lowered in the bucket and removing the thaw points for the first time, I filled the bucket with the thawed sand and gravel and Ed hoisted it and dumped it. Ed shouted down the shaft, "I just scraped up a handful of black sand and I can see gold all through it!"

"There's plenty more where that came from!" I called back.

During March and April mining operations had been carried on with few interruptions. The huge dump, black against the snow, stood out as a monument to our efforts. Pay dirt taken out in the winter must be sluiced during the spring and summer, when water becomes available. Beneath the surface, tunnels and drifts led in various directions, following the layers of black and ruby sand which prospected best.

One morning, while going about our work as usual, I was lowered in the bucket to remove the thaw made during the day before. To my surprise, I found the workings flooded with water. "We've run into thawed ground!" I shouted to Ed. "We're through!" Here was water sufficient for all sluicing purposes, within a few yards of the dump; the pumping plant set up, suction pipe lowered into the shaft, and sluicing could be started at once!

The task of hauling the heavy pumping machinery from the beach to the claim must be accomplished while the snow remained solid, for all must be moved piecemeal, by dog-team. The sluice-boxes and lighter part of the equipment were easily handled by our own dogs and sled, but a neighboring miner furnished a strong sledge and his own team of four dogs to augment our own team for hauling the engine and pump.

"The huge dump, black against the snow, stood out as a monument to our efforts. Pay dirt taken out in the winter must be sluiced during the spring and summer."   —Will

Steam thawers working at winter mining in Little Creek district, 1906. Mining companies brought huge machinery up from the states to thaw the tundra and stockpile sand for summer sluicing.

Storms
"The sea was a-roaring and the wind a-howling."

Cape Nome, Alaska
September 3, 1900

Dear Folks,

Well, the storm is even worse than it was and we are shut up in the tent like mice in a trap. We just have great times doing nothing. We had rice pudding and cottage pudding for dinner, served with whiskey sauce. We eat to pass away the time. We have singing too. Sing church hymns and play poker at the same time. The wind is blowing as the wind at Cape Nome can blow, and the rain is pouring down. The old stovepipe falls off and nearly blinds us with smoke, but we stand it as long as we can then rush for the door.

I wish you could see us now. We are a tough looking lot. Ed has on his old yellow coat and siwash cap and lots of bale rope whiskers all over his face. I still wear the old coat and vest, more from habit than for comfort as the buttons and buttonholes will not meet by about a foot. The sleeves are coming out at the shoulders and my waistband gave out long ago.

—Will

Scavenging the Prosper, *of San Francisco, wrecked by a storm in September 1900.*

The sailing ship Sequoia, *wrecked on the beach at Nome. "There are three ships wrecked between us and town. There is a large, fine, three-master near us on the beach."* —Will, September 1900.

Nome Indian Village
September 10, 1900

Dear Folks,
We have had a fearful storm and another one is brewing. All the plants are badly wrecked. Ed and I walked three miles down the beach and saw engines in all stages of dilapidation. Pipes are all broken and twisted and carried away.

There are three ships wrecked between us and town. There is a large, fine, three-master near us on the beach. There is not a barge or lighter afloat, all are beached. Launches and tugs galore line the beach. The steamers beat it out to sea and hove to; others went to St. Michaels, and others went out under the lee of Sledge Island, twenty miles out, and rode out the storm.

The sea was a sight to behold, boiling and rolling in mountains as far out as we could see. The sea came up almost to the tundra. Our pump and engine were just high enough to escape damage and we have our suction pipe out so we escaped damage.

We are the luckiest miners on the beach.

—Wilfred

"The sea got higher and higher, and washed the pump away from its base, and the pump weighs 800 pounds."
—Will

Nome, September 30, 1900

Dear Lulu,

Four days have passed since I started to write and Sunday is here again. Before we came to Alaska I was told that there were no Sundays here, but the time goes so rapidly that it seems like we have two a week.

We have a male quartet in our camp. We sing everything we know and have some pretty good music. Al sings a very good tenor and Tom R. carries the "chune." Ed helps Al, and I manage the bass.

We sing "The Old Oaken Bucket," "On Jordan's Stormy Banks," "Swanee River" and "Old Black Joe." The latter is our favorite; we sometimes sing it before we get up.

We have been living on fish for the past week. We have nothing to do but pick them out of the sluice boxes as the pump throws them out by the hundreds. They are tomcod and are from 5 to 12 inches long. The beach is being deserted now as everyone who has nothing to stay for is leaving. We have cleaned out nearly all of our grub so I guess we will have to get our tickets soon.

Well, I'll have to stop now as I have overdone myself. The tent is flapping in the wind and the rain is pouring. The sea is roaring and we are going to have more trouble, I guess.

Such is Sunday, September 30 at Cape Nome.

—Your brudder Willie

Storm damage along Front Street in Nome, September 1900.

"You never saw such a sight as the sea is this morning. The breakers come in like race horses and look like mountains." —Will

The wreck of the Ruby Richardson *on Nome beach, 1902.*

Cabin 101, Nome
September 11, 1902

Dear Folks,

When we went to bed last night at 9:30 p..m. there was no sign of a big storm, but at 10:30 p.m. the sea was a-roaring and the wind a-howling. We got up and put the tools and equipment high and dry and came back to bed. The sea got higher and higher and washed the pump away from its base and the pump weighs 800 lbs. The pump is turned over and half-buried, but the engine is all right. This storm equals the big storm of 1900—came clear to the tundra. It has washed out everybody on the beach.

—With Love, Will

September 12, 1902

They picked up a dead man just below us this morning. We saw him—he was murdered, I believe, and then thrown into the sea. He had a hole punched between his eyes that you could stick 3 fingers in and also the left side of his head was knocked in. It looked like he had been hit with a pick or some sharp instrument. He was a Swede—stark naked and no marks or bruises on his body. There were also several lives lost in the storm in town. There are lives lost in every storm.

They have a life saving station at Nome, but people take great chances. We do not take any chances at all and have no trouble. Such is life in the far north.

—E.J.M.

Home

"Our cabin is the best on the beach."

Nome, Alaska
June 30, 1901

Dear Lulu,

We stayed in town two nights and then got our freight and baggage from the *St. Paul* and towed it all out to the diggings in our boat. We took possession of the log cabin next to our shack —I wish you could see our home. Our cabin is about 16 x 20 inside. We have a four light sash with 24 panes in it for a window. We put in a board floor and have our stove in the middle of the room.

Ed and I slept two nights on our cots, and more miserable nights I never spent. We could not keep warm or lie comfortable.

Tom and I went to town and got a wool mattress for $6 and carried it between us on a pole for 6 miles to camp. It weighed nearly 100 lbs and took us 4 hours. We laid in bed until 8 this morning. We are just as comfortable now as if we were at home.

I bought a fine copper and nickel-plated tea kettle also. Also have an aluminum milk pitcher. We now need a broom very badly as our floor gets littered from chopping and sawing wood. How would you like to cook snow and ice for water? Well, that's what we are doing.

Did I tell you that we also have a thermometer and an alarm clock?

—Love to all, Wilfred

Ed enjoys a break from his labors outside the brothers' cabin. The number 165 identifies their mining claim.

The brothers, tired of living in a tent, bought Cabin #63 for $20 in 1901.

Cabin #63, Nome Beach
July 29, 1901

Dear Parents,

Did I tell you we bought our house? Paid $20 for it. You see we are fast becoming property owners. Our cabin is the best on the beach. Since we put a canvas roof over it, it doesn't leak at all. We now own two buildings, No. 63 and 63½. We have taken out about $500 but after paying for ground, labor and oil, we haven't a great deal left. I wish you could see our ranch. You would be surprised to see so much stuff. Tents, cabin, machinery and engines.

Don't forget the canned fruit. We'll send you some money, Mamma, to buy cans with. There is no comparison with cannery fruit. You don't know how good that jam is.

I am going to town tomorrow to pay for oil. I will send a roll of films with the letter. No steamers have gotten in so have had no mail for 2 or 3 weeks.

We are not getting fat very fast. We are well and able to eat as usual. We are living much better than we did last year. We have rice, eggs, macaroni, St. Charles Cream, maple syrup and baker's bread, besides jam, fruit. Fresh plums sell at 25¢ a dozen. Apples 3 for 25¢.

Well, it's 9 p.m and I must go to bed. Love to all,

—Wilfred M.

Ed hauls fresh water to the cabin from Quartz Creek.

Jessie with sled dogs at the Quartz Creek cabin, which was once one of the Palace Hotel roadhouse cabins. A mast from a wrecked ship served as the ridge-pole.

Jessie with sled dogs on the bridge Will and Ed built across Quartz Creek.

Tomcod was hung in the sun to dry for use as winter dog food.

Jessie does the laundry at the Quartz Creek cabin, summer 1904. She accompanied the brothers to Alaska on the day fter her wedding to Ed, on June 1, 1904.

By 1906, the brothers had acquired another cabin at Edwards Creek. Jessie decorated it with great style and ingenuity, as this view of the common room shows. Several Eskimo tools and toys grace the walls, as well as books, well-thumbed magazines, and mementos of home.

Jessie's bedroom wall in the Edwards Creek cabin was decorated with drawings and photographs of the Gibson Girl, a wildly popular feminine ideal of the time. The Gibson Girl wore her hair gracefully piled high, had a long, elegant neck, and wore a full skirt with a wasp waist and a white blouse with leg-'o-mutton sleeves. Jessie managed to achieve this style to a remarkable degree, even in the wilds of Alaska.

Neighbors

"They are a very curious people."

Golovin Bay, Alaska
July 1, 1899

Dear Folks,

    I am wearing mucklucks on my feet. They are made of walrus hide, waterproof, and come up to your knees. We put hay in the bottom of them as the sole is very thin. They are very light to wear, a good thing to tramp over the country with.

    The natives were trying to blow my cornet this morning, and they had a great time with it. They are a very curious people. If they can find a hole to look through, they will be peeping in the tent all the time. They want to come in all the time and I have to fire them out.

    They are a dirty set. They sit on the ground and have a pot of fish and they all eat out of it with their fingers—dogs and all. They are dressed in furs and calico.

    The natives have plenty of dogs. They feed them fish and they are fat. At night they howl like coyotes.

    You can read a newspaper the whole 24 hours here now.

    —Yours truly, E.J. McDaniel

Ah-ta-see-uk of Penny River, with a native boy, on a visit to the mining camp.

The Methodist Mission School at Sinrok Roadhouse, 26 miles west of Nome.
Back row, left to right: Lottie Renny, Jessie McDaniel, Reverend M. A. Sellon, missionary,
and Ed McDaniel. In the front row are native students.

Left to right: The wife of Ah-ta-see-uk holds little Wee-li-tuk; See-ya-uk, her son; two King Island girls; little Oo-ta-na and her mother, Ka-neel-uk (meaning reindeer). Will McDaniel made friends with the natives, learned their language, and recorded their names when he took this photograph.

> Nome
> September 12, 1901

Dear Lulie,

    I tried to take Uma-luk-tuk's picture the other day while she was shaping muckluck soles with her teeth, but she was modest and hid her face behind a tent. She was dressed in the latest style, red pajamas, walrus hide mucklucks and a fur shirt waist.

    I saw another with a blue skirt trimmed with accordion pleats, I believe, about a foot and a half wide. The tucks were red, white and blue, alternating.

    There are a great many Eskimos here this year. They come from up the coast as far as the Arctic and from the islands, Diomedes and St. Lawrence. They are trading ivory and mucklucks and drinking all the whiskey they can get.

    They go sailing up and down in the Umiaks, just as the wind favors them. They are a shiftless lot and take life easy.

    Well, it's 9:15 p.m. and bedtime, so goodnight. Remember me to the old maids, etc.

> —With love, Wilfred

Deserted Eskimo camp near Indian River.

See-ya-uk

See-ya-uk was an unusual boy, bright and friendly, contrasting greatly with the shy and retiring children of the Eskimos. He and I became great friends, and it was from him that I learned much of the life of the natives, and also something of their language, which I studied, enabling me to talk with them, thereby gaining their confidence. See-ya-uk, during his frequent visits, would often bring some native delicacy, a choice cut of seal meat, a bit of seal liver, or sometimes a fish or berries from the tundra.

I later became acquainted with his father, Ah-ta-see-uk, and also his mother. The following winter a little brother arrived in the family. He was named Wee-li-tuk. Ed always insisted that he was named after me, for See-ya-uk never could say, "Will," as I was called, but pronounced it "Weel."

"Tuk" is a diminutive suffix in Eskimo, meaning little or small; hence, Little Weeli! A year or more later, See-ya-uk told us that Wee-li-tuk had spoken his first word, an occasion of equal interest to parents, whether Eskimo or Caucasian. When asked what word Wee-li-tuk had spoken, See-ya-uk replied, "Ah-la-pa," meaning, "I'm cold!"

—from "Alaska Beckons"
Will McDaniel, 1946

Oo-ta-na and See-ya-uk, Penny River native children.

Eskimos

The name "Eskimo," or *Esquimau*, was applied to this widely scattered race by European ethnologists. The simpler form of the Danes, "Eskimo," is generally used in preference to the longer French spelling, *Esquimau*. The name is a corruption of a phrase or word used by two tribes of Indians, meaning, "those who eat raw flesh."

An Eskimo is never at a loss for a name for anything, even if it is something he had never used or seen before. To him, a stove is a combination of fire and iron and he calls it, *eek-no-wik*. *Eek-nuk* means fire and *sow-eek*, iron. By combining the first syllable of fire, "eek," and the last syllable of iron, "wik," and adding a middle syllable, "no," the result is "fire-iron."

The word "igloo," meaning hut, or house, I have never heard used by the Eskimos of Alaska. Their word for house, or dwelling, is "ee-nih," accented on the last syllable. Sites for dwellings are usually selected near a protective bank of earth or rise of ground along the seashore or rivers. Drift-logs, obtained from the beaches, are used in their construction, the earthen bank, faced with logs, frequently forming one wall of the hut. The roofs are of logs, covered with sod from the tundra. A small window or two, facing south, and covered with thin, translucent material obtained from the intestines of seal or walrus, furnishes a small amount of light. The huts usually consist of one room.

Fires for warmth and cooking are built on the earthen floor, the fuel being obtained from the accumulation of drift on the beaches and rivers. A chunk of blubber or fat is hung above the fire, from the ceiling, adding oil to the embers and producing a smoky flame and strong odor of burning grease. With the coming of warmer weather, tents are set up and summer camps made.

—Will McDaniel
San Jose, California, 1930

"See-ya-uk and I became great friends, and it was from him that I learned much of the life of the natives, and also something of their language." —Will

Eskimo girls in reindeer parkas: Jennie and Blanche (Nee-ok-see-nah), on the right.

The same girls: Blanche (Nee-ok-see-na), left, and Jennie in "Sunday Dress."

A Love Story

Nee-ok-see-na was an unusual girl. Above average in intelligence, she had had the advantage of attending a school for natives, under the direction of some early missionaries. She had a fair knowledge of English and could read and write well. The missionaries had given her the more pronouncable name, Blanche. She had beautiful, wavy black hair which fell almost to her waist when she chose to loose it from the two conventional braids worn, as is the native custom. Her features were regular and pleasing, with a display of white, uniform teeth; a smile any girl might envy! From "The Cape" to Sinrok, she was reputed to be the beauty among all the native girls.

Her lover, Tooni, among his people, was an outstanding young native, shrewd and ambitious. He lived in the native village at Penny River, making his home with a family who shared their hut with him.

Some two miles west, at Cripple River, Nee-ok-see-na lived with some of her people, in a similar village. Located as I was on the beach, about mid-way between the two rivers, I saw much of Tooni as he passed back and forth on his frequent visits with his beloved. He always dropped in for a visit and to discuss the affair closest to his heart!

One Sunday afternoon, looking down the beach, I saw a strangely garbed figure approaching which proved to be Tooni. He was clad in an outfit which, in his estimation, would settle any doubts about him still lingering in the mind

Tooni, a Penny River Eskimo, was Nee-ok-see-na's suitor.

of dusky Nee-ok-see-na! Proudly wearing a discarded military cap, he had also bedecked himself in a worn, misfitting coat and, beyond all understanding, had forced himself into a pair of boys knee breeches! A pair of ladies black stockings encased his ample calves, and on his feet, a pair of "out-side shoes."

Many trips took place between the villages before Tooni jubilantly announced, "Me ketchum!" Forthwith, he began making plans for domestic life, some of which, perhaps unknown to Nee-ok-see-na, included the making, on a large scale, of mucklucks, a labor performed entirely by the women. In a harness shop in Nome, Tooni had seen a leather-sewing machine, and he envisioned possessing a similar one, with its unlimited possibilities for turning out muk-luks.

In due time, the wedding took place, and Tooni changed his residence to the village at Cripple River, after which his visits to me became less frequent. Some weeks later, a sad and dejected Tooni stopped at the cabin.

"What's the matter, Tooni?" I asked.

"Nee-ok-see-na run away!" he replied.

Later I learned that Nee-ok-see-na had taken up her abode with an Eskimo family beyond Cape Nome. Efforts of Tooni for a reconciliation proved useless. It was many weeks before he submitted to the inevitable and became reconciled to the loss of Nee-ok-see-na and his dream of mass production of muk-luks.

—from "Alaska Beckons"
Will McDaniel, 1946

Nee-ok-see-na was "reputed to be the beauty among all the native girls." —Will

On the following pages are photographs of unidentified Nome natives whom Will McDaniel photographed in Nome, in a photographer's studio.

III

Cutting up a walrus: C. Madsen and H. G. Kaiser, photographer. Will often traded negatives with other photographers.

Eskimo graves at Quartz Creek, eighteen miles west of Nome.

Will's notes read: "Party boarding S. S. Victoria at East Cape, Siberia." —the legend on the photograph notwithstanding. The picture was taken from shipboard, as passengers were being brought out for boarding.

Siberia

"Small beginnings may take us . .
we know not where."

East Cape, Siberia
August 14, 1904

My Dear Lulu,
    Don't this letter look like I was quite a long way from home? We left Nome last night at midnight and reached this place at noon today. Have had a fine trip and everything strictly first class. When I left I did not expect to find anyone I knew but found a man who has come in every year with us on the *St. Paul,* so that we passed the time pleasantly.
    This a.m. we passed Kings Island and about noon the Diomedes and into the Arctic Ocean. The country is somewhat different on this side - more rugged and colder. The snow is lying on the coast and hills now almost as it was at Nome when we arrived. Have had sunshine all day and have taken a lot of photos. We did not go ashore, as the surf was too high to permit landing. The *Victoria* is a fine boat and fast. She is almost as large as the old *Zealandia*. Just imagine having watermelon in Siberia. Had some for lunch.

—Will

Landing in a launch from the S.S. Victoria at Uelien, Siberia, on the shore of the Arctic Ocean. "We now bow to the authority of all the Russias; Uncle Sam has faded away." —Will

St. Nicholas, Siberia
August 15, 1904

Dear Folks,

 We were unable to land at East Cape so came down the coast about 60 miles to this place and landed in a launch. Had a grand trip yesterday. The coast is cut up with bays and rivers and much more rugged than the American side. We took on two Cossacks and a Count yesterday.

 This a.m. three or four umiaks of natives came on board to trade, and we had all kinds of fun. A very thick fog came in so that we will not be able to get out until it clears. We expect to go back to East Cape and into the Arctic again.

 I bought a pair of small walrus tusks for a dollar, but had to have the Company agent to explain to the native what the money was for. He wanted powder and caps, so the agent explained how he could get them at the station with the money, and he let me have the tusks. I traded a pocket mirror for a bead bracelet but was unable to buy anything with money. They don't place any confidence in coin—they want sugar, flour, or trinkets.

—Will

Winter houses, built from whale ribs, sod, walrus hides, and rocks.

Native huts in Chukchee village, near the Arctic Circle, Siberia. 1904.

                                                Siberia
                                                August 16, 1904

Dear Folks,

    Left St. Nicholas yesterday at noon and started for the Arctic. Stopped at Graphile Station and went ashore in the launch, was among a favored few as all of the passengers did not land. Went up a large river for about a mile and then set ashore at a village. Did some trading. Money won't go here. Traded my old gloves and a blue spotted handkerchief for some curios. Took lots of photos and gathered a few flowers.

    This is the grandest trip of my life, and it is worth a whole season to take it.

    We steamed up to East Cape and unloaded some freight and then rounded the Cape and went into the Arctic up the north coast of Siberia and up to the Arctic Circle. Stopped at a native village called Whalin [Uelien} for half this day and are now going back through the Strait to Graphile again to get some of the Company men and then return to Nome. Have taken 2 and ½ dozen photos.

                                          —Love to all, Will

Bering Strait
August 16, 1904

Dear Folks,

    We arrived at St. Lawrence Bay this evening and picked up the Company men and about 25 natives, whom we left at their village, and then we turned northward again and are now making for Cape Prince of Wales. I will try to describe some of what I have seen.

    The natives of Siberia are different in many ways from the Nome Eskimos. They are better appearing, being lighter in color and better features. Their language is entirely different, so that it is rather hard to deal with them. The squaws cover their bodies and legs with reindeer skins, so that they have the appearance of being stuffed. Their legs look large as a sack of flour, and their bodies are as wide as they are high. They tattoo their faces and arms much more than our natives.

    The Siberians have some very peculiar customs, one of which is the trading of wives. When the men go from one village to another they exchange wives for the time. Woe be to the woman who changes husbands without the consent of her husband, as he often bites her nose off. Saw several with their noses missing.

    Another custom practiced mostly in famine years is the hanging of the old and infirm. The old people, when they outlive their usefulness, ask their nearest relative to perform the job. They have a choice of hanging, stabbing, or shooting. When the old folks get cranky and fussy they take them off and hang them anyway. There are no trees, so they put up three oars or a log and up they go.

    Their houses are entirely different from the Alaska native igloos. Theirs are built of ribs like an umbrella with the handle off and covered with skins. They are very large—20 or 25 feet across. There is a hole about four feet high by two feet wide to enter and for the smoke to go out, no opening in the top at all. They have their fire most anywhere and don't seem to mind the smoke.

—Will

Siberian Yup'ik woman in front of her winter home, Chukchee, Siberia, 1904.

Bering Strait
August 16, 1904

Dear Folks,

The Siberian coast is the most desolate and God forsaken place on earth, I think. At East Cape the mountains end with a perpendicular wall of rocks covered with pinnacles and crags like saw teeth against which the Arctic Ocean beats—and where the ice piles up to a great height. In the gorges the snow and ice never thaws.

The villages are located on the little beaches usually at the mouth of a river, and scattered along about ten or twenty miles apart. They use whale ribs in place of wood for framing and building, boats, and net racks. Wood is almost unknown—no drift wood at all.

They seem contented & happy, you always get a smile when you crawl into their house. We were met at St. Nicholas and given a royal welcome by the chief. He was a funny looking old man with scraggy whiskers and with a thing like an eye shade on made of skin. His clothes were of skins entirely and he looked for the world like Mr. Skin clothes of *Examiner* fame. He greeted each of us as we landed with a hand shake and a loud "Hello." He felt very important; I guess they never saw such a sight before.

The *Victoria* has a steam siren, and every village we would pass they would let it loose. The natives must have thought Old St. Nick was aboard.

Well, must stop and get some sleep. Expect to be in Cape Prince of Wales and then start for Nome.

—Good Night, Wilfred

Yup'ik grave made from whale ribs, rocks, wooden posts, carved fish, leather strips, near Chukchee, 1904.

Sundays

"Let's go wildflower hunting!"

September 19, 1905

Dear Folks,

Last Sunday we went up to Otter Creek in the hills and fished. Had the finest trout fishing I ever had. I caught 15 trout from 8 to 15 inches long and had great sport landing them with a split bamboo pole. The big fellows were very gamey and vicious.

This is the country I have been looking for and have found at last. Trout fishing and hunting and plenty to eat.

With love to all, I am affectionately,

—Wilfred

Opposite: Jessie and Lottie Renny, who worked at the Sinrok Roadhouse near Nome.
"We gathered geraniums, lemon-yellow poppies, phlox, birdseye, cream cups, fragrant blue and white forget-me-nots, and big blue violets." —Will

Jessie, Ed, and sled dogs on the tundra near Nome: "*We picked cotton grass, cowslip from the pools, iris and bluebells from the marshy places, and monkshood and harebells from among the tundra grass.*" —Will

Brook trout from the Otter Creek tirubtary to Cripple River. "Had the finest trout fishing I ever had. I caught 15 trout from 8 to 15 inches long and had great sport landing them with a split bamboo pole." —Will

Lottie Renny wades into Cripple River: "At the river, Lottie's quick eye saw a huge salmon . . . Wearing gum boots, she was able to run out in the river and grab it by the tail." —Will

Flowers and Fish

One beautiful morning in early summer, Jessie, my brother's wife, said, "It's such a beautiful day, we ought to go wildflower hunting on Cripple River." [Lottie], a new friend, was a young lady who had just come in from the States. Jessie had the lunch packed when we returned.

On the tundra, we picked cotton grass, cowslip from the pools, iris and bluebells from the marshy places, and monkshood and harebells from among the tundra moss.

"When do we eat?" [Lottie] asked. "I'm getting a terrible appetite!"

"Just a few miles more and we'll reach the river," Ed said. "Then we'll eat."

At the river, [Lottie's] quick eye saw a huge salmon struggling to get into deep water. Wearing gum-boots, she was able to run out in the river and grab it by the tail! She held it up while I photographed it; then she let it go in peace.

Later, we went to the mountains and gathered geraniums, lemon-yellow poppies, phlox, birdseye, creamcups, and fragrant blue and white forget-me-nots, and big, blue violets which had no perfume. It is here on the hills that the reindeer moss grows. In the winter the reindeer paw the snow from the ground, to uncover the moss and feed upon it.

When we reached home we were very tired, but felt well repaid for the trouble we had taken, and we all agreed that an Alaskan picnic was as nice as anyone could have.

Story told by Wilfred McDaniel
to his daughter, Irene, 1932

Nome, Cripple River
September 19, 1905

My Dear Lulu,

Your letter came yesterday, and I was very glad to hear from you as I am disappointed when I do not get a letter from you. Suppose you are having plenty of warm weather yet. Here we are wearing furs and trying to keep warm.

Did you see the Eby girls when you were in the city? She has not answered my letter yet. Guess I am in for another arctic winter all by my lonely. Those Alaska winters drive some crazy, others to matrimony, but I am going to put it off as long as possible.

Miss Renny comes down quite often and helps break the monotony. She says they are going to have a piano this winter. I'll grease my old fid and maybe make a killing, don't you think?

—With love and kisses, Will

Lottie Renny, in mucklucks, waterproof sealskin boots made by natives.

Will, Lottie and Jessie enjoy an Alaskan picnic.

Lottie washes Will's face at Cripple River.

Ed and Jessie at the Sinrok Roadhouse, 26 miles west of Nome. "Sinrok Charlie" stands at right with dogs.

Will and Lottie on Cone Mountain, viewing tundra and the Bering Sea. "The morning is warm and sunny, just like California weather in May. The distant mountains are white with snow and the dark blue Bering Sea makes a grand picture as it sparkles in the sunlight." —Will

Lottie beside the geodetic survey target on Mt. Rodney. "Viewed from a certain perspective, the mountain resembles a woman carrying an infant on her back and followed by a dog—representing a native woman who so left her husband and was turned to stone as punishment." —Will

Arctic twilight—at midnight—on the tundra near Nome.

Cripple River
September 18, 1905

Dear Lulu,

We received our last mail today, only one letter for me, that was from Mrs. Stewart. I have felt rather neglected this summer by everyone. I put up two jars of blueberries and one of cranberries this morning and tomorrow I will try mossberries. We have been having mossberry pies on Sundays and think them fine. All other berries are scarce. Flowers gone, too. You would never know there ever had been any here. We have had two snows and it freezes ice every night. The boys have on their fur caps for the first time this year.

I was in hopes Rev. Herrold would come up this winter. It will be so lonely and we are looking forward to a very fierce winter, so I shall be shut up alone most of the time. It is too bad for me out today, and I can stand a great deal, so I am putting in my time writing.

I have your book of flowers all done, ready to put the covers on. I have also one for our cousins Lulu and Edith. Everyone here wants one who sees them, but people here can make them for themselves.

I am sorry you are having so much trouble with your eyes. Are you going to pack and face prunes this winter? Don't forget to write to me. Love to you all.

—Yours lovingly, Jessie

Jessie with sled dog pups at the Cripple River cabin. "I think the pictures of the little dogs are good, but yours spoils the picture. You look bad, and I feel like crying to look at it. I do wish you were here to help me fix up when I move, but come soon, as you can not stay there another winter. Life is too short to spend it that way." Written to Jessie by her mother, Mrs. J. W. Drake, September 1906.

October on the beach, just before the Bering Sea freezes over.

Winter
"Cold is no name for it."

Nome, Alaska
October 11, 1900

Dear Folks,

 Well, the arctic winter has set in and the "white silence", as it is called, will shut off this part of the earth from the outside world for six or eight months. The steamers are coming in for their last trip and we must soon get off or else stay. We expect to go out on the *Ohio* to Seattle. She is billed to sail October 15th, but as she is not in yet, it is probable she will not get off before the 20th.

 Since October 1st, it has been one continual storm, rain, sleet, snow, and the wind blowing a gale all the time. The wind blew all night and sleet has been falling today. It cuts one's face and hands like shot as the wind drives it along. Cold is no name for it.

 We have made about three hundred dollars. Now just keep this to yourselves. The black sand tales are a fraud. Only one kind of black sand carries gold, and the gold bearing black sand is mixed with the barren black sand at a ratio of 1 to 1,000. It would take 1,000 tons of the concentrates to yield one ton of gold bearing sand. We get about 100 lbs. of black sand at a clean-up so you see there is nothing to it.

 I have been sitting on the woodpile hugging the stove and trying to write. The wind is blowing and the snow and sleet come in gusts. Tent life is getting too uncomfortable. We think the fare out will be about $40 or $50, second cabin. Steerage is $25. I think most of the fellows go steerage as they can save a few dollars, but we have had enough of that.

—With love, Willie

September 19, 1905

Dear Mother,

    I will write tonight as there is a vessel going out in a day or two. We received father's letter of August 28 and Lulu's of a few days earlier. They came in on the *Ohio*.

    The weather took a sudden notion to freeze up a few days ago and now we are having regular winter. Have had a fierce gale from the north and it is exceedingly unpleasant. Skating will be good in a day or two if it keeps on. The tundra is frozen hard and the water has stopped runing in the ditches. We are having the weather we usually get the last of October. Last night we had a fine aurora, another indication of the freeze-up.

    We bought a cabin from a native for $20 and have torn it down and are now putting it up on the claim. Today we dug a cellar and got part of the floor laid. We will have a comfortable cabin and we will not have to walk through the cold and snow to get to work. I am anxious to get to thawing.

    Things are booming out here. Heard yesterday that two claims across Penny River were bonded for $30 thousand a few days ago. Everybody on the old beach line is feeling rich but me. I am sort of a pessimist; when I see it I will feel rich, too. Some are feeling rich though they haven't even raised any color. It looks to me like we are going to realize our reward for our years of work and come out ahead at last.

                                                                —Will

Ed and Jessie skating on Penny River.

Ed and sled dogs, Penny River.

The Freezing Sea

"Today is November fifteenth," I remarked. "The ice is usually on time."

"We had better stay on the beach today; that's worth a whole winter to see," Ed replied.

Everyone keeps their eyes turned seaward at this time, for the coming of the ice is a sight never to be forgotten.

A twinkling of sunlight on the distant horizon is seen, far to the westward. No ice is yet visible.

"Here it comes!" Ed shouted. As the hours passed, a faint, white line appeared, slowly creeping shoreward, from the west, in the current of the Bering Strait. At nightfall the sea was whitened near the horizon, as far as one could see, and only a few miles of open water between shore and ice were now visible.

During the night the boom and crash of the moving ice became louder and louder, and at daybreak, when we looked out, we seemed to be in a strange world. No sound of breakers could be heard, the sea was gone! A great, rough white plain had taken its place.

Under pressure from beyond, ice nearest the shore grounded in the shallow water and the huge, thick floes stopped momentarily, then from the impelling force behind, slid forward over one another, tumbling and splintering, forming the numerous pressure ridges paralleling the coast - a rough, broken mass of green and white.

After another day had passed, all was quiet. No movement of the ice could be seen, no sound broke the stillness. "The Great White Silence" had taken over.

from "Alaska Beckons"
Wilfred McDaniel, 1946

The common room in the Edwards Creek cabin, 1906. The decorated tree is a small, leafless willow bush. There are gifts and chocolates on the table, and a small skull, capable of mechanical tricks. The magazines and books have been read and reread many times.

Christmas in Alaska

DECEMBER TWENTY-FOURTH came, clear and still, the thermometer on the outside wall of the storm-room registering in the thirties below. That the Spirit of Christmas would not be lacking, a small, leafless willow bush was placed on the table and decorated with such few ornaments as were obtainable, and covered with green paper trimmings in lieu of foliage! Gifts were placed under the tree in the usual manner, and our Christmas Eve was complete in every detail.

Christmas dawned, crisp and clear with no change in the weather. Our Christmas dinner, as we had planned, was to be roasted ptarmigan, and the birds had been placed in a sack and kept on the roof of the cabin, frozen, and safely out of reach of our dogs. The birds selected were first placed in cold water to thaw, the feathers were then removed; cleaned and stuffed with dressing they were baked in the oven. Cranberry sauce from our supply of canned goods, sweet potatoes and corn from the same source, completed the menu, while ice-cream from the canned milk supply, frozen in snow and salt, provided the dessert.

Christmas, here in the North, was the one great day in all the year. Coming at the mid-winter season, when daylight was at its lowest ebb, it gave opportunity for all to enjoy a period of rest and relaxation. Even the Eskimos caught the spirit and many an igloo was brightened by the gifts of sugar and tea from their white-skinned neighbors.

On the day following Christmas, Ed and I decided to haul a wood supply from the beach, where we had piled it during the summer, for winter use.

Several trips had been made with the dog-team, and the wood pile at the cabin was growing steadily. The logs were rough and ice coated, many being crusted with sharp, frozen sand. We had decided to haul another sled-load of logs before sundown, which at this season occurred about 1:30 p.m.. A sudden fall in temperature came as the sun slipped under the horizon, and it was not until then that my hands felt extremely cold. Handling the rough logs had gradually worn away the canvas mittens, allowing the snow from the wood handled to enter the small holes thus formed, melting from the warmth of the hands and creating dampness within.

I swung my arms in the customary fashion to start the circulation, and as the discomfort of the cold disappeared, attempted to tie the lash ropes over the sled-load of logs. Being unable to do so I called to Ed, who was some distance away.

"Come and tie the lash ropes," I shouted. "My fingers are numb!" I shook off my mittens, to find my fingers a waxy white color, creeping steadily downward until fingers and thumbs were changed completely to a hue similar to that of tallow candles. Unable to replace my mittens, I waved my arms about, calling to Ed, "My hands are frozen, hurry and do something!" He rushed to help me, grabbing some snow and proceeded to rub my hands with it. This had no effect whatever, and the line of yellowish white crept steadily lower. Fortunately, not far distant was the cabin we had previously built and now used as a cache, or store-house.

Hurrying to the cabin, Ed quickly started a fire in the stove and then gave his attention to me. Kerosene had been recommended for frost bite, but none was available. A quantity of engine distillate was stored in the cabin, and Ed poured some into a gold-pan and I immersed my hands in the liquid. The sub-zero temperature of the distillate only made matters worse, so Ed resorted to friction, rubbing my hands vigorously with his own, while the fire in the stove gradually warmed the temperature in the cabin.

Slowly, the waxy white color began to recede and as the natural color returned, intense pain accompanied it. So great did it become that I fought off his efforts to help me, but in a few moments a deathly nausea overcame me and I was helpless to resist! Within an hour the thawing out was completed, the nausea had gone, and I hurried across the tundra, while Ed finished the loading and returned to the cabin with sled and dogs. The warmth of the cabin caused the return of the intense pain, and only by placing my hands in cold water could relief be obtained. My hands, now badly swollen, were coated with vaseline and bandaged, but there was no sleep for me that night!

The morning following, Ed removed the bandages, to find my fingers badly discolored and a mass of water blisters; three finger nails on each hand

Jessie in reindeer hide parka, fringed with wolverine fur. "We are looking forward to a very fierce winter, so I shall be shut up alone most of the time." —Jessie

being loosened and raised by the blisters which had formed beneath them. The pain gradually subsided and was soon gone completely; no movement of the fingers and thumbs was possible above the knuckles of the hand. Many problems confronted me after losing the use of my hands. Chiefly among them were dressing and eating. Buttons were an impossibility!

Christmas over, all looked forward to the coming of the new year, after which the old routine of mining and prospecting would be resumed. The road-house at Penny River was to be the scene of a neighborhood gathering on New Year's Eve, with dinner and entertainment. Helpless as I was, nothing in Alaska was allowed to interfere with pleasure during the long Arctic nights. At the appointed time, clad in muskrat parkas and muk-luks, we arrived for the celebration of the evening. With the thermometer at forty below, my hands again became very painful and it became necessary for me to stop at the Eskimo village on the way, for relief. The native woman in the igloo where I stopped kindly complied with my request for *oo-na-tuk emuk*— hot water—and by placing my hands in it, the pain soon left.

[At the road-house] Our genial hostess seated me next to her attractive young niece, who had but recently come in from "The States." She took a kindly interest in me, cutting my food and looking after me. If I was a bit more clumsy and helpless than usual, it passed without comment, and I missed nothing of the sumptuous dinner. Later in the evening a neighboring miner brought forth a fiddle and with accompaniments played by the young lady on a battle-scarred piano which had evidently strayed far from its usual environment, the evening passed pleasantly, with music.

Many weeks passed before movement of the finger joints returned. Serious sloughing away of skin and tissue occurred, the six nails, with the exception of thumb and first finger, loosened and fell off. New nails gradually appeared, skin and tissue was restored. However, complete as the recovery seemed, the effect of the freezing was never completely overcome, for during the many years that have passed since that day, something has been lacking in the usefulness of those six fingers.

Above: Lottie and sled dogs on the frozen sea at Nome. Lottie is standing on a pressure mound of ice.
Below: Will and Ed, with an eight-dog hitch, move 1200 pounds of mining machinery.

Jessie with a sled load of tomcod dog food..

The inclination of an unbroken dog, newly in the harness, is to pull frantically, exerting himself to the utmost, or to lag behind, resisting the efforts of the dogs ahead to haul him along! Becoming weary of either extremity, he soon learns to take his share of the load, and all goes smoothly. The lead dog knows the commands—gee and haw—turning to right or left. A well trained team, at the command—Whoa!—stops immediately, and when given the order—Lie down!—will do so instantly, never moving until the command—Mush on!—is given.

from "Alaska Beckons"
Wilfred McDaniel, 1946

Edward Creek cabin, February 1905. "How strange it seems, and yet we know how true it is, that here we are enjoying summer heat, with green fields, gardens decorated with flowers of summer, orchards in full bloom, while our dear absent ones are locked in the strong embrace of an Arctic winter."
—Written to Will and Ed by their father, J.J. McDaniel, March 5, 1905.

Lost in the Snowstorm

IN EARLY MARCH, Lottie, coming from Penny River on her skis, arrived early for a day's visit with Jessie. Soon after mid-day, a south-east wind sprung up, the sun became obscured by haze, and loose snow whipped up by the rising wind blew like smoke over the white landscape. So sudden was the change, that Jessie and Lottie - in the cabin - failed to notice that a severe storm was in the offing. Late in the afternoon Lottie decided to return home, but the scudding clouds of snow precluded the trip on skis. Fearing that her folks would become uneasy at her absence, Lottie declined Jessie's invitation to remain for the night.

"Will! Get the dogs harnessed and take Lottie home!" Jessie called to me. Hastily, the team was harnessed and Lottie, clad in reindeer parka and hood, with extra blankets, was stowed in the basket of the sleigh. From our cabin to Lottie's home at Penny River, the distance was less than two miles. We followed the well packed and well marked trail from the cabin to the beach. Along the ice strewn beach, the trail was rough and once the sled struck a hummock and overturned, but fortunately, Lottie, tightly wedged in the basket, was not dislodged. The sled was quickly righted and the journey to her home ended without further mishap.

As I took the trail for home, the whirling clouds of snow had now shut off the little remaining twilight, but I was sure that the dogs could be depended upon to find their way back. Quickly covering the trail along the beach, I halted at a driftwood pile at the edge of the tundra and faced the direction of the cabin. The stinging snow was brushing my right cheek and I decided that by keeping the wind against my cheek, I would arrive at the cabin. After covering half of the distance, I noticed that the wind was now blowing against my back: the dogs were drifting with the wind, not seeming to sense the direction of the cabin. The leader, Nancy, would, at command, "Gee!" pull to the right, but would soon drift back with the wind. I halted, placing Nick in the lead, but he too turned the team so that the gale was at their rumps, the line of least resistance.

I now fully realized that in drifting with the wind I had missed the cabin. Stopping, I thought I saw some familiar objects not more than twenty yards

Ed and Jessie picnic on Mt. Rodney at fifteen below zero.

A miner's cabin is almost buried under snow and ice.

away - a pile of sluice boxes I hoped, but it proved an illusion, a scrubby willow bush merely a few feet away! Turning the dogs about, now facing the storm, I attempted to urge them on, but they refused to face the gale. As a last resort, I could lie down with the dogs and with blankets over us, I might stay alive, but I decided to take the lead harness myself and guide the dogs back to the beach. Again on the beach trail, the behavior of the dogs changed and they seemed more anxious to keep going, so I climbed into the sled, certain that the dogs would stay on the beach.

After a time, I noticed that the trail was becoming uneven, the sled rising and falling over snow covered hummocks. A sudden encounter with a huge ice barrier brought a halt, and, to my amazement, I recognized the undulating surface and hummocks as the snow covered pressure ridges, far from shore, on the ice covered Bering Sea!

Leading the dogs as before, I made my way back to the beach and located a telephone pole. I decided to retrace my course by following the telephone poles, hoping to locate a neighboring miner's cabin. I made my way from pole to pole and at last, a gleam of light ahead!

I knocked loudly on the door.

"My God, Will! Is that you?" he cried.

With a rush the dogs were inside before I could enter and the sled jammed in the doorway!

The flying snow, dug up from the snow-covered tundra, filled the air with a swirling, blinding cloud of white, shutting off the meager daylight and blocking out all vision beyond a few yards from the cabin. The temperature dropped to thirty-five below. Had the cabin been constructed of logs and sod, as were the igloos of the Eskimos, the interior warmth would have been retained much longer. But it was built of sawed lumber. The Arctic gale dissipated the heat from the thin walls so rapidly that the fire in the stove had to be kept at a high heat. The water barrels which stood close to the stove froze over.

Front Street, Nome.

At the end of the second day of the blizzard the wood supply had shrunk to a low ebb. We donned our muskrat parkas and huddled close to the stove, later sleeping in them. Morning came with no let up in the velocity of the wind, and the temperature was at forty below. Outside, the snow had drifted high around the cabin, and the dogs, housed in a tent close by, were content to lie in their straw beds, the tent almost covered with snow. We managed to fling them a supply of frozen fish each day. The poor fuel from the beach was about exhausted, so we decided to drag a sack of precious coal from the boiler.

Toward the end of the third day the gale diminished. The hundred pound sack of coal was completely gone. Snow melted by the heated stove pipe formed icicles along the eaves, not hanging in the usual perpendicular formation, but standing out at grotesque angles from the force of the wind.

from "Alaska Beckons"
Wilfred McDaniel, 1946

Nome winter residents on skis and in parkas. Thousands of miners left Nome in October and returned to the States until May, when they again sailed for Nome.

A native neighbor hunting seals on the frozen Bering Sea.

Will poses proudly in the car he bought with gold from Alaska—a 1906 Sunset, made in San Jose—on the family ranch.

Epilogue

In October of 1906, Jessie received word of her father's failing health, so the brothers hastily closed their cabin and accompanied Jessie to California on the last ship to leave Nome that year. The three Sourdoughs, flush with success, bought first-class tickets back to San Francisco, which gave them private cabins, beds, heat, and dinners of "roast goose and fresh strawberries." Only Will returned to Alaska in the spring of 1907.

Will wrote, "In 1908, we bonded our holdings to a ditch company then being organized in New York City. In the fall of that year I bade farewell and made my final trip to the Great Outside. The panic on Wall Street in 1907 ruined the money market, the ditch company failed, and our deals were never completed."

Ed, Will, and Jessie resumed their lives in San Jose. With their gold money, the brothers paid off the mortgage on their parents' ranch, and each got started in the building trades, contracting and building homes in the Santa Clara Valley.

Ed and Jessie had two daughters, Esther and Ruth—both of whom still live in California and have given their blessing to this book. Jessie died in 1947, Ed in 1951.

Will remained a bachelor until two days before his fortieth birthday, when he married Ada Bayley, the organist at the Christian Church in San Jose. He presented her with a wedding ring cast with the last of his Alaska gold. They had two children, Wilfred, Jr., and Irene, both of whom live in California. They have actively sponsored this book.

Will wrote articles for the *Alaska-Yukon Sourdough News,* and attended annual Sourdough reunions in California. In this way he kept in touch with many old friends, including Lottie Renny, the woman whom he had first met at the Sinrok Roadhouse near Nome, and who appears in several photographs in this book. Six years after the death of his first wife, Will married Lottie. She died in 1950, and Will died in 1954.

The beach at Nome, where Will, Ed, Jessie and Lottie looked out at the Bering Sea.

Alaska- Yukon Sourdough News.
June 1, 1946
Will McDaniel

GOLD! GOLD! The Klondike—Nome! During those hectic days of the late 90's, like wildfire, the news spread across the nation and beyond. Men sacrificed, endured the untold hardships of a new frontier—cruel to many, lavish with her treasures to others.

At the great gathering of Sourdoughs just held in San Francisco, one heard little mention of gold. The lure which called those hardy adventurers to the North seemed to have little place in the atmosphere of comradeship and good will. Men and women met again to renew old friendships and recount the old, but ever new experiences over the years long past.

The poke, lean or plump, is no yard-stick to measure the friendships among those sturdy men and women of the early days in the North. Something finer, more enduring is theirs. The GOLD? Most of it has long since taken wings—all but forgotten. In its place, something far more precious has replaced it, something not to be taken away or lost—memories of our fellow travelers down the trail of life.

"More to be desired are they than gold, yea, than much fine gold."
—Psalm 19:10

Previously published by Scottwall Associates:
95 Scott Street, San Francisco, CA 94117
Telephone (415) 861-1956

Big Alma: San Francisco's Alma Spreckels
by Bernice Scharlach

Lincoln Beachey: The Man Who Owned The Sky
by Frank Marrero

Hometown San Francisco:
Sunny Jim, Phat Willie and Dave
by Jerry Flamm

The Farallon Islands: Sentinels of the Golden Gate
by Peter White

Pioneers of California
True Stories of Early Settlers in the Golden State
by Donovan Lewis

Mount Tamalpais: A History
by Lincoln Fairley & James Heig

California Heartland
A Pictorial History of Eight Northern California Counties
by Sandra Shepherd

San Mateo: A Centennial History
by Mitchell Postel

The San Francisco Fair: Treasure Island, 1939-1940
by Patricia Carpenter & Paul Totah

History of Palo Alto: The Early Years
by Pamela Gullard & Nancy Lund

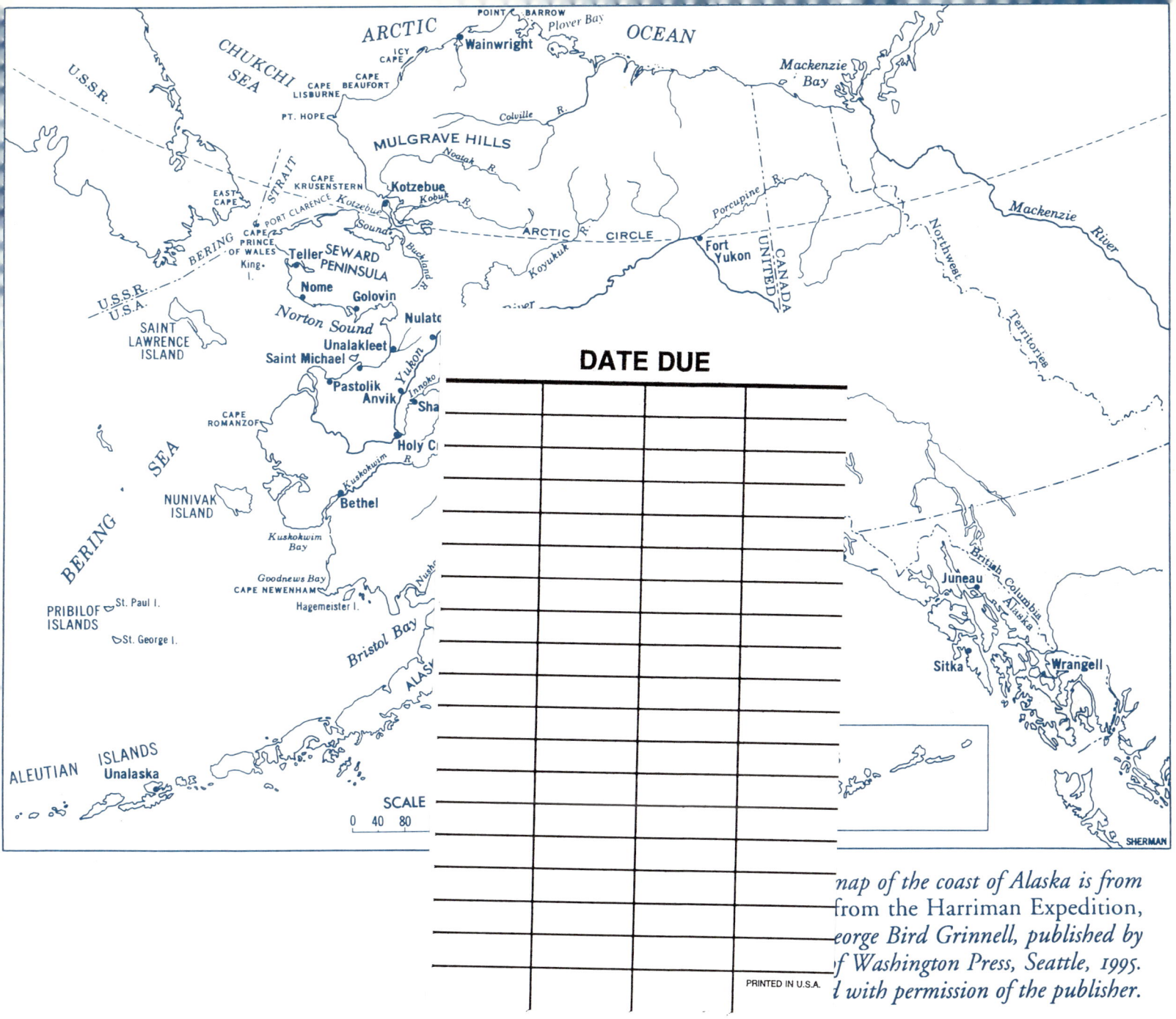

Opposite: detail from a map of the North Pacific, published in 1875, showing the powerful Alaska current flowing southward along the California coast. Ships bound for Dutch Harbor on Unalaska Island had to fight this current most of the way. Courtesy of the United States Maritime Museum, San Francisco.